May Your Swash Never Buckle

John C. Hendershot

Home of Arrrrrticulate
Christianity

May Your Swash Never Buckle
ISBN-13: 978-0-692-17646-7

Text copyright © 2018 John C. Hendershot
All Rights Reserved

Cover Design by Megan Welch.

Dedication

*To the memory of Charles Hendershot,
my grandfather, whom I never really knew.
He was an outstanding Bible teacher,
and an example to me.*

Acknowledgments

- My wife Betty, whose patience with this insane project has been utterly exemplary. She also appears in any number of the anecdotes within.
- My daughter Rebekah, whose professional editing skills have greatly improved the appearance and content of this book. (The errors remain my own.)
- The Legacy Coalition, a Christian group dedicated to the matter of Christian grandparenting (https://legacycoalition.com/) and in particular their representative at our church, John Coulombe. They were the ones who gave me the idea to write this book.
- Dwight D. Eisenhower, whose book *At Ease* provided me an example of the format for this book. This has prevented you, dear reader, from struggling through an amplified version of my resumé.

Contents

Army 11

Business 23

Church 35

Marriage 45

School 57

Eye Patch 69

Other 75

Family Ties 87

Quote Unquote 97

Of Influence 105

Foreword

It is the height of vanity (or arrogance) for someone who has led as dull and boring a life as I have led to then write his autobiography. Such an outrage requires some sort of explanation.

My defense in the matter is this. Some time ago, the Legacy Coalition, a Christian group dedicated to Christian grandparenting, suggested to its listeners that they should write their autobiography for their grandchildren. The suggestion struck home with me largely because my grandchildren live in Delaware but my wife and I live in California. We get to see them at most twice a year. There are a few things that I felt good to let them know. That's why I wrote this book. Of course, given the content, it will be some time before they get to read it. As of this writing none of them have yet arrived in their teens, so their copies will be put aside until a more appropriate time. But, dear reader, you might take inspiration from this. After all, if dull and boring amateur writer can produce this kind of a book, so can you — and probably do a better job of it. Your grandchildren just might appreciate it.

The title of the book requires explanation. If could a look at my picture, you would see that I wear an eye patch over my right eye. Every five-year-old in the country knows, without the slightest doubt, that this makes me a pirate. I'll save you the stories until later in the book, but I should point out that a man with an eye patch never needs a name tag. The expression used for the title has been around for quite a while, but just picture it this way. I make balloon animals. Sometimes, if requested, I make a balloon sword for somebody who really wants to be a pirate. The kid has to be dubbed into piracy, of course. So I end that little session with, "I hereby declare you to be an official pirate, junior grade. May your swash never buckle!" Now you know.

The style of the book may require a little explanation too. When I first started on this project I thought of it as being nothing much more than an expanded version of my resumé. This immediately surfaced the problem: I have a very boring resumé. So I rummaged through my mental attic, looking for a solution. I found one in an unusual place: Dwight D. Eisenhower. Yes, I mean the president. In his retirement he wrote a very unofficial sounding autobiography. Titled *At Ease*, it is a collection of stories that he told to his friends. Most of them were from a time before World War II; had he not achieved fame in that war, they would've been the war stories of a career soldier. So, inspired by this, I started to write down stories I would tell to my grandchildren. After I had the stories pretty well completed, I began to organize them into particular sections. As you can imagine, some of them don't fit in any particular place, so they are where you find them. For most of them, I added either "the moral of the story" or an appropriate verse from the Bible.

It's probably a good idea to tell you at this point that I am a Christian. Not just a church attender, I am an orthodox (note the small "O"), catholic (note the small "C") Christian. I believe what most Christians of most places and most times believed. I take it seriously, and to the best of my abilities have tried the live the life that Christ would prescribe. Of course, my efforts are imperfect. But please do not attribute to hypocrisy that which may be explained by stupidity, laziness or ignorance. Grandkids, you got my best effort. But I'm not perfect.

The actual act of writing this book produced some interesting revelations. The first one is just exactly how poor my memory is — and how invaluable it is to have your wife look over your shoulders at these things. Like many other creative works, it took on a life of its own. I found it necessary to add two sections to the book at the end. One of them lists a number of familiar expressions used in our family which might amuse you. I identify their sources, as much as possible, and give you an idea how we use some of the pet phrases we like. In addition to that I thought it might be useful to you to see who, among the writers of the world, has been most influential to me. There may be some surprising names on that list to you. But, as Sherlock Holmes once said, I trust that time doth not stale nor custom wither mine infinite variety.

I should point out for those of you who are thinking of doing something similar that I have taken advantage of a product known colloquially as "Dragon." This is a software product which converts speech to text. Professional writers are expected to be able to type at a furious pace. I type at the same speed that would be achieved by the average octopus. It should also be noted that the octopus would be more accurate in his typing. Hence Dragon. If you look it up on the Internet, it would be listed under "Dragon Professional Individual."

As the book is essentially an anthology of stories — very short stories — the reader might find it most useful to read this book a little bit at a time. You're getting the chocolate sauce on the ice cream of my life; consume responsibly.

Army

Introduction

Let's put it this way: The Army is a great place to be from. If you're a child growing up, when your dad leaves the Army, it's good news. You don't have to move every year, you don't have to start searching for friends every six months — you can be normal. If you can be rehabilitated, that is.

If you're in the Army, your number one objective is usually to become a civilian again. Either way, you suffer the ambiguity of leaving something of value. Military brats tend to find their toy chests a little thinner than most civilian kids, but the military does teach you a set of values that are very much neglected in the civilian world today.

- You learn the value of patriotism. Unlike the civilian, you're not taught that American history is just a series of horrible mistakes. You learn the value of liberty, and the price paid by those who fought for it.
- You learn the value of obedience. Today's society teaches you rebellion as the prime virtue. (They don't label it a virtue, of course.) Obedience is essential to teamwork, and teamwork is essential to accomplishment.
- You learn the value of hard work. It does not come as a surprise to you when you find that you must work hard to get something you want. In fact, what surprises you is that other people think that hard work is something that is terrible.

My experience in the Army came in two varieties. First, I was a military dependent. That means that your best friend is somebody you've known for maybe three months. You learn quickly how to carry yourself as the outsider. Every time you got into a new school, five or six of the bullies got together to beat you up. If you complained about it, your parents were told that it was your fault — "He just needs to learn to get along better with the other boys." You learned how to live the life alone.

As a soldier, I had it made. I had the dream assignment of every soldier in the Army. Because I was stationed at the Navy Postgraduate School, I didn't have to wear a uniform. I was working on some cutting edge statistical research, with a group of excellent people. And my number one priority was to get out on time and be a civilian again. Fortunately, my military experience had prepared me for a job as a computer programmer in the aerospace industry. So, with no further preliminaries, here are my tales about the Army.

Rubber Tire Dummy

During basic training in the United States Army we had to take bayonet training. This is just a little bit on the silly side, since most of us would prefer to use bullets rather than bayonets. But the Army thinks that bayonet training makes you more aggressive, so we all engaged in bayonet training. The method was relatively simple: someone had constructed a dummy composed of a large rubber tire and several pieces of rubber to make it look vaguely human. You were to run up to the dummy and stab it and slash it in an appropriately aggressive manner.

The first few attackers did as they were told, but as the rubber tire dummy never fought back our enthusiasm for this quickly waned. The drill sergeant in this exercise was one who particularly disliked me. I had a Master's degree and he had flunked out of college, which seemed to be all the reason he needed. Just before it was my turn, he stopped everyone going through and chewed us out for not having the proper aggressiveness. He evidently thought that I would just simply go along with everybody else. Not with an opening like that!

I charged that dummy with a scream that would've done a Japanese suicide squad credit. I stabbed, I slashed, I poked and mostly I screamed at the rubber tire dummy — "Die! Die! Die!" I slashed and stabbed the dummy to the point that the entire company was rolling on the ground laughing. There was obviously nothing the drill sergeant could do to blame me for this; I was just following instructions. He kept yelling, "he's the first man who's done it right!"

Moral of the story: Follow your instructions carefully. Even if it sounds crazy, follow the instructions literally. You might just get a good laugh out of everybody else.

Who's in charge?

I will never forget my first meeting with Col. Richard A. Robinson. He had just been assigned to our psychological research unit. He called all the programmers into his office and was dismayed to discover that not one of us was in uniform. I explained that we worked at the Navy Postgraduate School, which required civilian clothes so that rank would not interfere in the classroom.

He asked me who was in charge at the school. I replied that there was a civilian professor in charge of the computer facility; he said he was looking for who was in charge of our outfit. To be specific, "who is the OIC." (OIC stands for Officer in Charge.) I told him there was no such person. He then asked for NCOIC (Non-Commissioned Officer in Charge; i.e. sergeant). I told him there wasn't one of those either. At this point he lost patience completely and screamed, "well, who the —string of obscenities here — IS in charge?"

I replied, "Well, sir, I guess I am."

He promptly threw everyone else out (they left smiling at the thought that I was going to get whatever it was that was coming, not them). He then made me what I thought was one of the better offers you could ever get in the Army:

"From now on, troop, you don't guess you are in charge. You ARE in charge. You keep that computer off my back, and I'll keep the Army off yours." I had encountered a reasonable man! For the next 2 years I kept that machine off his back, and he did his best to do the same with the Army for me.

Later, as I matured, I realized the sense in what he had done. We were working with no one particularly in charge — which meant that decisions concerning things we argued about might have to be made by someone who knew nothing about computers. More than that, I found that once you realize you are in charge, things go more smoothly than if you're trying to figure out who is in charge.

Moral of the story: It's not that one leader is better than another; it's that one leader is better than two, or a committee. If you're in charge, be in charge.

Bugle Calls

Most of my early life was spent as an Army brat. Some of the places were bleak; the Army isn't very good at picking out garden spots for a military post.

But one assignment that sticks in my mind as the best fort I was ever on, bar none, is Jefferson Proving Ground. It was located on the Ohio River in the southern portion of Indiana near a town called Madison. To give you an idea of what appealed to me, this was the time when Davy Crockett was an absolute craze. Davy Crockett had a log stockade kind of fort. So did we. The GIs on the post tended to have less to do than was optimal, and they got together and built this log stockade/fort about 50 yards out my back door. Add to this the fact that JPG was the last post in the Army to run on *live bugle calls* - yes, with a live bugler - you can see why this place seemed to be ultimate level cool to a ten-year-old kid.

When we arrived at JPG, they taught us about unexploded ordinance. To convince us that we hadn't really seen this level of explosion before, they gave us a little demonstration. They put a can of C4 explosive on a slab of concrete. Then they marched us to the other end of the parade ground, which was easily the length of a football field and then some. They set off the explosive, and all our curiosity about explosives immediately evaporated. The stuff you see in Hollywood is trivial, because it must be small enough to fit on the screen.

We did, however, occasionally get the chance to go out onto the firing line. It amused some of the crews there to let us pull the trigger on things like a 155-mm cannon, or 50 caliber machine guns. It probably kept us out of worse trouble, too.

The place was a collection of farms that had been fenced in during World War I, so we had apple trees and berry patches to pick. I can remember my mother making jelly out of all sorts of berries. We were there less than a year, but I always thought it was the best place we had ever lived. In my later years, my dad told me that it was the worst assignment he had ever had.

He got the assignment by trading assignments with another finance officer. The one he was originally scheduled to get would have required him to parachute into the jungles of Laos, transport 300 pounds of gold to a French hotel in the capital city, and then use it to pay off tribal leaders for their opposition to the Communists. The other guy was single; dad was married with 3 kids, so they managed to persuade the Army to swap assignments. The other officer was never heard from again.

Moral of the story: Sometimes wonderful things come along. Enjoy them while you can.

Five Chickens

While I was in the Army, we attended a local Baptist church. I was asked to be a counselor to the high school youth group going up to a camp for a snow retreat one year. That Saturday I was playing a game of chess with one of the boys when five other boys approached me.

They announced that they were going to throw me into the pool. Why the pool hadn't been drained of water I do not know, but it was surrounded by a chain-link fence. It was clear that the camp managers did not want anybody in that pool. What was also clear was that I didn't want to go into that pool.

One thing that I knew, however, is that when five teenage boys approach you with something like this you are looking at five chickens. If one or two of them had approached me, I might've had some concern. But five of them were obviously a collection of people trying to encourage everybody else.

I got up, announced that I was going to throw all five of them in the pool, and then I said, "Starting with you." I grabbed the ringleader and started to hustle him outside, but he broke free and started running off into the snow. I never did get any of them into the pool (cooler heads prevailed).

Moral of the story: You don't get courage from a crowd. Courage grows from within.

Forest Fire

Believe it or not, I once put out a forest fire.

It happened this way. I was driving through Monterey in one of the more wooded sections of town. I noticed a fire just starting out. It was a line of flames that was perhaps 15 to 20 feet long. I stop my camper, grabbed my fire extinguisher, and discovered why it is that professionals don't use a fire extinguisher on a forest fire. A teaspoon of water would have had about the same effect.

I got on my CB radio and contacted the fire department, which immediately dispatched someone to the site. In the meanwhile, I took out an army entrenching tool (World War II surplus, from my dad) and proceeded to dig around the fire. I threw the dirt from the trench onto the fire. That seems to have handled it.

The firemen arrived, thanked me profusely, and taught me a lesson. One of the guys put it this way: "the first 2 minutes at a fire are worth the next 2 hours."

Moral of the story: Solve the small problems quickly so they won't grow into big ones.

Hi Archie

One of our lifelong friends is Maggi Mathey. We have many stories about Maggi, but perhaps the most interesting one concerns the time that I picked her up at the local airport. She was in the process of getting a divorce, and the proceedings for it were in Santa Ana. She therefore had to fly down and back each time she went to court. She asked me if I would pick her up at the airport and take her back to her apartment, which was the one just below our apartment.

Now, what happened next was a matter of appearances. It happened that I was teaching, as a volunteer, at a Christian school in Watsonville. In those days teachers wore coats and ties, and I was dressed in my best sport coat and tie. Maggi, who had been a fashion model, was dressed in a light knit dress which was extremely short. So, you have to picture the two of us walking through the airport, presenting the picture of me in coat and tie following the cute blonde. We walked right past the preacher's best friend, Archie, who ran one of the rental counters there.

Thinking nothing was wrong, having nothing to conceal, I simply said, "Hi Archie." The look on Archie's face did communicate that something was wrong. We, after all, attended a Baptist church. Archie drew all the wrong conclusions from this. Maggi and I realized there was nothing we could do about that. When we got home, Betty was arriving at the same time. We told her about it and she burst out laughing so hard that we had to practically carry her upstairs.

We had all sorts of fun imagining what's going to happen when the preacher comes over to remonstrate with me. We had it all arranged that Maggie would bring her 6-week-old baby up and let everybody's imagination run on from there. However, nobody ever called. We did get some unusual questions, though, from those who were informed 2nd or 3rd hand. Gossip was a problem in that church, and you must remember that you don't have control over what other people are talking about.

Moral of the story: Given the chance, people will draw the worst of conclusions from any set of circumstances. Be prepared for it, or at least be prepared to enjoy it.

Nate Burleson

Nate Burleson was a ghetto loser from Detroit. The judge gave him a choice: three years in the Army or two years in jail. He selected the Army. He went through basic training and into combat still dependent on drugs, taking life and war as lightly as possible. His object in life was to be either drunk or high all the time. As you can imagine this didn't make his advancement in the Army very easy.

One day Nate had a life changing experience: his best buddy died in combat there in Vietnam. That caused him to think like he had never thought before. He finally made up his mind, and went into the company commander's office (unbidden), saluted and asked the captain what he had to do to make sergeant. The captain simply pointed at a chart on the wall which outlined the requirements for promotion to each grade level. Nate looked it over, turned around and saluted the captain again, and said, "thank you, sir."

When I met Nate, he had already turned things around. He was struggling with a group of computer programmers when he had no knowledge of computers. He left us mostly alone, but we knew if we had to deal with the Army, we could go to Nate. He was a fine example of an enlisted leader. When he left us, he got an assignment in Hawaii at the rest and recreation center for combat veterans of Vietnam.

What impressed me most, though, was the Army's reaction to Nate. The route to making sergeant was posted on the wall. If you look at it the way I do, you see this is a rather rough and impersonal form of forgiveness. The Army wasn't really all that concerned about what he had done in the past; he had decided to change his future. The Army was ready to accept that change – and it's a rare civilian organization that is as ready as that.

Moral of the story: People make mistakes. Forgiveness is a necessary skill in human beings. Be prepared with a method of forgiveness, and people like Nate will seek it.

Mess Sergeant

One of the things that most soldiers of my generation remember is KP. That means working in the kitchen, usually cleaning up. I was pulling this duty on a mess hall that was open around the clock so that those who are on duty at night could take a break and get a meal. Somehow I had managed to anger the Mess Sergeant, and he assigned me to the duty of cleaning the coils on the back of one of the refrigerators — something that is rarely done and obviously was intended to put the young soldier in his place. I realized that the sergeant wanted to go as soon as anybody else; his girlfriend was waiting outside in the car. So, I very carefully took my time to polish those coils to a state of shining perfection. That didn't please him at all, so he came by to chew me out again.

But I was ready with an answer: "Sergeant, there is in theological circles a place of eternal confinement for the condemned; may I suggest that you find your next duty station there?" The sergeant went away to try to piece out the meaning of this rather formal statement.

He eventually came back and said that he had figured it out, and as he told me what bothered him was not where I had told him to go — but that he was going to have to be a cook there. We got along fine after that.

Moral of the story: If you must tell someone to go to hell, do it with class.

Pearls

My father was stationed in Japan for about three years. During that time he enjoyed an unusual status among the Japanese. Dad was a finance officer; he was the guy who paid the troops and kept the books. As such, in Japanese eyes, he was a banker. This doesn't sound too important unless you know that in Japanese eyes bankers outrank military men. So, when he went to the officers' club he always got the best booze (and paid for it.)

This had another interesting effect. At that time military officers could get a Japanese maid for housekeeping purposes at a very low price. The maids lived in a dormitory and were assigned by the Japanese to the various officers. No one gave much thought to the fact that our maid was named "Ichi." The name is Japanese for the number "one." In other words, dad had the highest-ranking maid in the dormitory.

This would probably have gone without notice until the day that my mother decided she was awash in surplus cloth diapers. My sister had just become potty trained, an event usually accompanied by several repetitions of the Hallelujah Chorus. Paper diapers didn't exist in those days, so you had to wash the cloth ones. Military families usually didn't haul things like that around once they had served their useful purpose; the government is not accustomed to shipping surplus weight. So, mom looked around for someone to take the diapers. Since Ichi had mentioned that her sister was pregnant, mom offered them to her. There was a little reluctance to take them, but the language barrier kept it from being clear why such resistance might exist. The diapers were duly transferred.

Apparently Ichi was better connected than we thought. Shortly thereafter my father was called into the general's office and told that his contribution of diapers was greatly appreciated. So greatly appreciated, it was cause for the Japanese to return the favor. Dad was instructed to go to a particular pearl merchant in Tokyo to receive this gift.

When dad got there, he was rather nervous as he looked at the merchandise in the window. The pearls were all excellent quality, and the strands of pearls being displayed in the window were priced at over a month's salary for a captain in the Army. Dad went in, met the proprietor and complimented him on the pearls in the window. The elderly gentleman in question said that of course such pearls as that were not fit for such circumstances as this. He went into the back room of the store and opened a Mosler safe that could've come out of somebody's Western movie. The pearls — the proprietor gave him two sets, one for my mother and one for my sister — were stunningly gorgeous. Dad asked him for a price. The old gentleman would not take a dime; it was a gift.

I don't know how much those pearls would be worth today; I do know that when my mother had me take them to a jeweler to be restrung, the jeweler in question was quite specific: "if you ever want to sell these pearls, please call me first." My sister still has her set, as far as I know; my daughter, I believe, has the other set that used to belong to mom.

Apparently, for we never really found out for sure, our maid Ichi was very well connected to the royal family of Japan. The gesture was considered significant because it came from an American army officer's wife to a woman in Japanese society. This being just after World War II, it may have been viewed as a gesture of friendship.

Moral of the story: Do what is good and right without hope of reward, and God will sometimes surprise you.

Business

Introduction

CS Lewis once remarked that there was a great difference between the way men and women describe themselves. Suppose you ask a man at a party, "what do you do?" You will almost invariably get an answer that describes his employment. If he has a recognized trade or profession, you'll get something like, "I'm a plumber" or "I'm a doctor." Otherwise he will try to describe his job to you. Ask a woman the same question and you'll get an answer which could come from anywhere. It's usually not her job that describes her, it's her cats, quilting, activism, church or any number of other things. This difference very often drives differences in performance. Men are expected to lie, cheat, steal, slash, burn and any number of other villainous things to get the next promotion. Women are expected to be nice.

Very few businessmen would take Paul's advice to be content in their current station. For the most part, as long as the current station wasn't completely intolerable, I was content to take his advice. My example was my father. He stayed in the Army for twenty years and rose all the way up to major. He was not, by many people's standards, a roaring success. But he never evaluated himself on the basis of when was his last promotion. He had more important criteria. He passed those criteria on to his son — me. So, let me give you the warning: if you think your business life is the most important thing you must deal with, you have seriously underestimated what the world will do without and what God would like you to do without.

In writing this section, I became aware of something that probably has always been true, but I didn't notice it before. That is sex — that is to say, the number of times that sex comes up in business when you would think it would not. Never having been the tall dark and handsome type, in retrospect I am surprised by the number of women who wanted to have sex with me. I am also surprised at the number of times when sex was used in a manner I considered completely unprofessional. They tell me things have changed; I'm sure they have. But the role that sex plays in business probably hasn't lessened in importance. Don't be surprised when it comes up; be prepared. Know who you are; know whom you love and be loyal to the love of your life. As we told our kids, you should have sex with your spouse on your wedding night as your first-time experience. Do it God's way the first time - it works.

Making Friends

One of the earliest, rudest and meanest managers I ever worked for was a fellow by the name of Rich. He thought he was a genius, particularly when it came to math. He had, at best, a high school math education and on numerous occasions I was obliged to try to persuade him that his brilliant mathematics were in fact wrong. I endured a great deal of verbal abuse from the man, but as he was my boss's boss I pretty much had to put up with it.

One night I came home grousing about it to my wife. She looked at me with that look that says that I have not been thinking, and then said to me: "why don't you try making him your friend?" She was right, of course. That's the Christian thing to do. It just seemed a little impractical at the point. But she went on: "whatever you are doing now, isn't working. You might as well try something different."

So I did. The next morning I went in and, as I passed Rich in the hall, stuck out my hand for his and said, "Good morning Rich!" He was dumbfounded. He knew how to manage an antagonistic relationship, but someone trying to be friendly with him was a new experience. I persisted for some months in doing this; every chance I got to be his friend, I took.

A little over a year later I got a sign that something was taking effect. I no longer worked for him, but my job included making some presentation charts for him on occasion. He came into my office and was obviously desperate. I realized that, if I wanted to, I could give him an excuse for not giving him this work when he needed it, but just an hour or so late. I didn't do that; I immediately got to it and gave him the charts he needed in time. He actually said, "thank you." A rare occurrence in his life, believe me. After that time I found that while Rich was never really a friendly person, the antagonism was gone. On several occasions in my new job he supported me in business meetings.

Moral of the story: The Scriptures tell us to turn our enemies into our friends. That's not altruistic; that's practical advice.

"You have heard that it was said, 'YOU SHALL LOVE YOUR NEIGHBOR and hate your enemy.' "But I say to you, love your enemies and pray for those who persecute you, so that you may be sons of your Father who is in heaven; for He causes His sun to rise on the evil and the good, and sends rain on the righteous and the unrighteous. "For if you love those who love you, what reward do you have? Do not even the tax collectors do the same? "If you greet only your brothers, what

more are you doing than others? Do not even the Gentiles do the same? "Therefore you are to be perfect, as your heavenly Father is perfect.
  (Matthew 5:43-48)

Intimidation

One of the changing points in my life came when my boss called me into his office and told me that one of my employees complained to him about my conduct. I was puzzled by this, so I asked my boss what the problem was. He answered me that I was intimidating her.

I exploded. I told him that I don't intimidate people, don't like being intimidated, avoid intimidation and otherwise could not see the point. His reply was very revealing: "John, you're the most intimidating man I've ever met."

I just couldn't handle that answer. I told my boss I was going to take off early and think about it and I'd pick up the subject again the next morning. On my way home I fumed about it. It was a hot day, the car air conditioner didn't work, and I was in traffic with the windows rolled down. I began to think about it this way:

I'm not intimidating; I don't intimidate people. Now, if you want intimidation — my dad! There is intimidation! Company commander in the Army, jumps out of airplanes with two pistols blazing, the kind of guy who would file court-martial papers on a two-star general (and did) — there's intimidation!

And then it hit me: everybody says, "You're just like your father." It was quite a revelation, and motivated me to change the way I was doing things.

Moral of the story: Knowing yourself is not easy but is easy to neglect. Take the time for self-examination.

Coffee Pot

Have you ever heard the phrase, "lesson without words?" Here's a good example.

Rich, who was my boss's boss, was up in the executive lounge where I happened to be going over some presentation papers. He went over to get a cup of coffee, poured it, and put the now empty pot back on the burner. One of the secretaries, female, told him that he was supposed to make the next pot of coffee.

He exploded. He proceeded to give her a lecture, half screaming, that we had secretaries to make coffee, not executives like him. But, as he was doing this, his boss came in — he was a corporate vice president. He saw what was going on, went over to the coffee pot and proceeded to make a new pot of coffee in the pot that Rich had just put down. He waited for it to finish, took a cup and walked out without mentioning a thing.

Moral of the story: Leadership is often best done by example.

Sexual Harassment

One of the things you never want to hear in your business life is your boss telling you that you're being investigated for sexual harassment. When he told me that I was rather shocked. I know what sexual harassment is, and I knew that I hadn't done it. I also knew that I was working for a company that would consider any woman's complaint of sexual harassment to be the equivalent of being convicted for it.

The word got around. I wound up telling my team — about thirty-five people — that if they were asked about it they were to tell the truth, the whole truth and nothing but the truth. This saved my bacon.

About a month later, the two women involved in this (my accuser and her manager's manager) left the company. No explanation was given, but I felt I was lucky to have them go. It wasn't exactly luck.

About three years later I got the story from somebody in personnel. In the middle of this fuss, we had been outsourced from one company to another. The new company took this allegation very seriously and sent out a personnel person from headquarters in Dallas to investigate. By the time she got there the story being told had been embellished quite a bit, and her reaction was that we needed to get all the ducks in a row to take it to the El Segundo Police Department for criminal prosecution. This made the two women rather nervous, but given what was going on they couldn't back out at that point. A thorough investigation was done. What they found was this: on the day I was supposedly sexually harassing this employee, I was actually in Chicago working on an installation. They had seven or eight witnesses to this effect. They closed the matter by suggesting to the two ladies that they would really like to look for work elsewhere.

I'm not sure of the moral of this story. It's either that honesty is the best policy, or that God sometimes is looking after you in ways you'll never know.

Invisible People

One of the lessons my father taught me while trying to turn me into a good Christian gentleman was this: the measure of a Christian gentleman is how he treats the invisible people.

What does that mean? The invisible people are those people who must be nice to you, or they'll get fired. That includes flight attendants, clerks behind the counter, people over the phone — any number of people who are "professionally polite." If you treat them as human beings, are calm with them and allow them to do their job the way they've been trained, you not only get better results but you keep your blood pressure down too.

Moral of the story: As they say in the movie business, be nice to the little people on the way up. They'll be nice to you on the way down.

This Hose, Doc?

One of the more interesting characters I have worked for was J. Webster Daly. Known as "Doc" because he was a retired physician, he was as opinionated as most men will ever get. He had been John Wayne's doctor, along with a lot of other Hollywood celebrities. His retirement business was making industrial x-ray machines and renting them out to the aerospace industry. One of my duties was to go along with him when a machine needed to be repaired. It was usually the very large transformer that had gone awry, so we would get somebody with a forklift to take it out and put it on our truck, then haul it away to the engineering shop that fixed them.

It was a summer job for me, and the hours were intermittent. One night he called me up and asked me to go with him to replace one of these transformers. We got in the truck and went down to the site. Now, disconnecting a transformer is not entirely a clean operation. The unit has a pair of hoses from a cooler. One of these hoses was always under pressure pumping oil in; the other hose was the return hose. When you turn the cooler off to disconnect those hoses (done with a pocket knife) it's important to cut the return hose and let that little bit of oil drip into a bucket rather than cut the hose under pressure.

I climbed a 20-foot ladder to get up on top of the unit reached over and with my pocket knife in hand I asked Doc which hose to cut. He answered, "the one on the right."

"Your right or my right?"

"The one in your left hand."

"Doc this hose feels awfully hot — I think it's the pressure hose."

"Cut that hose!"

So, I cut that hose. Transformer oil began to spray all over the place. It's rather sticky. You don't want to spray it all over your x-ray room because it's a bear to clean up. The foreman for the x-ray lab was screaming obscenities at me, and I was rather glad to be 20 feet in the air where he couldn't get at me.

Doc told me to go out and wait in the truck. I sat there waiting with the hope that I would be able to get a ride back without being fired first. All I would need at this point would be to have to call my parents and ask them to come get me. About half an hour later Doc and the guy with the forklift showed up and put the transformer on the truck. Doc jumped into the cab on the driver side, slapped me on the knee and said, "I like you, kid! You do what you're told, when you're told, how you're told."

A little while later I got the explanation. In those days, x-ray machines exposed a plate of film which then had to be developed like an ordinary photograph. This meant that there was a dark room and lab in the x-ray facility. The foreman of this x-ray lab was in the habit of taking X-rated pictures of his girlfriend and distributing them to various other men. Doc was a firm believer that pornography had no place in business. Apparently the two of them it had argued about it before, and Doc decided to do something about it.

Moral of the story: Do what you're told, when you're told, how you're told.

Meeting Like This

Her name was Sherry. She was a sunny, clean scrubbed girl next door type (and devout Mormon) who just oozed friendliness.

One day I was walking down the hall in the office with my nose stuck in some computer print out. As I came around the corner I ran squarely into Sherry, who was carrying a large number of things she had just copied. Being much the larger, I knocked her down.

Have you ever had one of those moments when you wished you knew what to say right at the exact time? This was one of those moments. As I helped her pick up her things, I said to her, "Sherry, we've got to stop meeting like this." It's an old joke, but she loved it and giggled profusely.

It became a password between the two of us. We would go past each other in the hall and whisper, "we've got to stop meeting like this." We thought it was just so much fun — until one day my boss stepped in.

He called me into his office and began a tirade about men who conduct an affair in the office without even the decency of renting a motel room, making no effort to conceal it, and so on and so on. I kept nodding my head in agreement, telling him he was exactly right, because I thought he was talking about his boss (who was a notorious philanderer.) He finally got so frustrated with my lack of understanding that he blurted out, "I'm talking about you and Sherry."

I burst out laughing. When I finally managed to contain my giggles, I told him to give Sherry a call and ask her to step in to his office. She did, and when I explained what had gone on she got the giggles too. We finally managed to make it clear to him that it was simply a joke. It shows you, however, how things can get distorted all out of proportion in a business environment.

Moral of the story: Do you think the worst of other people? That's what they're thinking of you.

Roar of Typewriters

There are many ways to get rid of people in your company. Most companies take a straight and direct approach; if there's a layoff, they announce it first and then go about telling individuals that their services are no longer required. There's usually a little politeness that goes with it, telling them how much we'll miss them. But for the most part it's a straightforward action.

Sometimes, however, the company is in the situation where it wants to get rid of a lot of people but doesn't wish to directly fire them or lay them off. That happened to me in one of my first jobs. After the man who had founded our division died, corporate headquarters sent out a retired Air Force general (with a reputation as a hatchet man) to take over the division. His method was quite ingenious.

I remember being called into the office of my manager's manager one Friday. I was the junior programmer in the department; he was trying to persuade me to take the position of manager of data processing at our subsidiary in Houston. I wasn't too enthused. The afternoon was getting late and we agreed we would talk about it again on Monday.

On Sunday I got a call from the man. He assumed that somebody had told me what had occurred already. I confessed my ignorance and he let me know that I was now the highest-ranking man in the department. Everybody above my position had been fired over the weekend; some of them didn't know it yet. They found out by coming in at 9 o'clock Monday morning to the general's office and being handed a pink slip. They were told they had one hour to leave the building or be arrested for trespassing. My manager's manager was not only told he would be arrested for trespassing, but they had him clear out his office on Saturday accompanied by an armed guard, with the gun drawn, who had been told that this man was a psychotic ex-Green Beret.

This had been planned quite a bit in advance; three weeks earlier we had been given a notice that all the locks would be changed in our facility and that no one was to come in that weekend. My department was absolutely destroyed; the others were untouched. But the general had made his point. He announced at the 10 o'clock meeting that everyone there had a job and that if they continue to perform well, they would continue to have a job.

Nobody believed him; everyone thought there would be another Pearl Harbor as soon as he could arrange it. The roar of typewriters doing resumés that afternoon was deafening.

Moral of the story: When money is involved, the sneaky, dastardly, most offensive maneuver is probably preferred. Watch out for it.

Did We Offend?

There are certain things that you just don't think of as being a typical interruption. Most people don't think there might be an earthquake today. Most days, they are right. On this day we were not so lucky.

We were having a videoconference with London. This is not like Skype today. In those days you had a television studio with seats in a fixed position and cameras pointed at the correct angles so that all you had to do was turn it on and have the other fella turn his on — voila! You saw him; he saw you and business got done.

One of the things that was uncomfortable about doing this came from the fact that the studio was on the thirteenth floor of our building. In Southern California, if you have something like that up in the air, they require that you bolt everything down so that it doesn't fly around and hurt someone during an earthquake. So, we were sitting in chairs that you couldn't move behind desks that wouldn't move. Even the cameras were bolted to the floor. This had an interesting side effect.

We had just reached a point where we began to talk about the financial responsibilities. It was a typical business discussion; they thought we charged too much and we thought they were paying too little. Things got a little bit sticky in the discussion when the Whittier Narrows earthquake hit. All of us being good California boys, we ducked underneath the desks. All at once.

What we hadn't figured on was the fact that everything being bolted down meant that the people in London would see no shaking. All the stuff shook together. They could not tell that we were having an earthquake; it appeared to them that all of us had suddenly decided, simultaneously, to duck beneath the desk. There was a silent pause, after which we heard a plaintive voice from London say, "I say, old chaps, did we offend?"

Moral of the story: Sometimes your earthquake is their puzzle. Make allowance for the fact that the other guy may not understand your circumstances.

Houston Oaks

One way to learn the lesson of how to behave while you are a business traveler is to experience "the best steak in Texas."

We had a situation where two of our competing vendors supported one of our subsidiaries in Houston. My boss gave me explicit orders that I was to do absolutely nothing to offend either of them, as they were the only technical support our subsidiary had. So, naturally, when one of them invited me out on Monday night I went with him. I found out Tuesday morning that everything that went on in that conversation was well known to everyone in the plant. Tuesday night the other vendor took me out.

It wasn't until Wednesday night that things got a little interesting. The first vendor invited me out to dinner that night, and decided that since I wasn't too impressed with dinner Monday night this time he would take me to the best steak in Texas. The place in question was the Houston Oaks Hotel. Everything went fine until the waiter asked if I would like to see the wine list. I said yes, and he brought out this huge, cowhide covered wine list. It had exactly 3 wines on the list: Gallo white, Gallo red and Gallo pink. I smiled and handed the wine list back to him and asked for a beer.

The word got around the plant the next day that I laughed at the wine list in the Houston Oaks. True, to a point, but none of the people at the plant had ever dined there either. Thursday night it was the other vendor's turn and he decided that the problem was I was from Los Angeles and therefore terribly cool and sophisticated. We made the tour of every strip joint in Houston. By the time we got to the last one my eyes had long since glazed over and I just wanted a cup of coffee. We came back to my hotel to have breakfast.

The waitresses had not yet come on duty, so the cook came out to take our order. He was a large, burly black man. He carefully wrote down what the other two guys were going to have — the champagne breakfast. I ordered ham and eggs and, "coffee — lots of coffee."

The cook looked at me, looked at the other guys with disdain, looked back at me and said, "Right! Us Baptists have to stick together." The romance of business travel quickly faded away after that.

Moral of the story: You are the same person on the road as you are at home. Act like it.

Church

Introduction

Let me be clear with the perfectly obvious: Jesus Christ is the most important part of my life. The reason God is going to let me into heaven is the sacrifice that Jesus Christ made on the cross. If you want to know the rest of my theological thinking, there is a website with twenty some odd years of lessons on it which portrays my thinking quite well.

As a result, church work is something I take very seriously. As of this writing, I have thirty-seven years of experience in teaching the Bible to adults. As you might imagine, I think this is important. But it's also important to remember that while the topic is important, the teacher is just another part of the body of Christ.

However, that doesn't mean that church life is smooth and slick, following the regulations carefully. In fact, some strange things happen in the church, as you will see in this section.

Well Qualified

There is only one qualification you must meet before you can become a Christian: you must be a sinner first. Some of us (blows on fingernails, polishes them on shirt) are exceedingly well qualified.

U Dummy U

It takes a little while in your marriage to understand that your wife has cosmic powers of which you are not even aware. It happened this way.

In a fit of overextended ego, I took the position of an elder in the small Christian church which we attended. My first meeting coincided with the first meeting of our new chairman. He came in with an agenda of items that he wanted fixed right away. At 1:30 AM he brought up his last item. He did not like the organist playing background music during the delivery of communion; he felt it interfered with contemplation. We were quite willing to pass anything he wanted at that time, but he insisted on full and fair debate, so it took us to 2:00 o'clock in the morning to finally decide that we would no longer have this music.

The organist, who was the minister's wife, was quite well aware of the feelings and had been accommodating them by playing one Sunday and not the next, using her artistic judgment to decide on any given Sunday. For the next two Sundays we did not have music during communion. Thinking all was well, on the third Sunday we heard her play. My brain snapped into the instant mode, "Oh no, a church fight!" We investigated after the worship service, and found that she had never been told anything of our decision. She was quite upset. Our chairman of the board took full responsibility for that and apologized to her. I went home wondering why on earth her husband had not told her about this.

I shared that thought with my wife, who responded by giving me the "you dummy you" look. This is the look the wife gives you when she thinks you should obviously have figured this out while you have no clue. I finally broke down and begged her to explain what that was all about.

She looked at me and said, "Sue is a gossip. Don't you think Chuck has formed the habit by now of never telling her anything that goes on at church?" She had looked into their marriage and saw that it must be, and assumed that I would do the same. I hadn't even contemplated it.

Moral of the story: Your wife knows by instinct that which you cannot calculate. Pay attention to her words.

White Dresses

As a deacon at a small church, and the newest one of the deacons, I got the short straw in several things. One was the task of rounding up eight men who were willing to wear a coat and tie in August, in Southern California, to serve communion. Tradition! A coat and tie in August in Southern California might just be considered something along the lines of suffering for Christ — at least mildly. Try as I might that one Sunday I could not find eight guys to do it.

So, I talked to the youth minister about this, and he couldn't see any reason why my idea wouldn't work. I recruited eight high school girls to do the job. I asked them to show up in modest white dresses with a very serious attitude. Nobody noticed what was going on until the girls walked in with the communion trays. There was an audible gasp from the congregation.

Of course, there was an emergency elders meeting immediately following the service. However, I knew that there was no place in the Bible which explicitly forbade women to carry communion trays. And considering the weather, they were much better dressed for the occasion. So, I went down in that church's history as a landmark of theology and practice.

Moral of the story: Sometimes it's easier to ask forgiveness than it is permission.

Is He Mad?

We arrived in Killeen, Texas (and joined a local church) when my brother turned five years old. As was my father's custom, Jim had his first chance to sit with the family in "big church." My father was a soldier; his approach to discipline was to yell at people. That included his children. We learned at an early age that the proper response was to stand at rigid attention, eyes straight ahead, until he finished his tirade. You then said, "yes sir" and went on with your life. My brother Jim was quite well aware of how to do this.

When he got into big church for the first time, he fidgeted through the first half hour of the service as five-year-olds will do. However, when the preacher opened his sermon, Jim's behavior changed. Our preacher at the time believed that a good sermon opened with the volume level about triple forte, crescendoed for twenty-five minutes, ending with a rhetorical question which was to cause you to contemplate your soul in mortal dread and terror. He then decrescendoed back down to triple forte for the next five minutes, the choir would sing a hymn and the congregation would leave, thankful to have escaped the fires of hell for another week.

When the pastor opened, Jim's eyes immediately locked on the pulpit. For twenty-five minutes he did not squirm or fidget or even move. But when the pastor got to his rhetorical question and dread silence, Jim looked over at my dad and in a stage whisper you could hear all over the church asked, "Is he mad?"

Moral of the story: Gold is where you find it. Embarrassment sometimes finds you.

Altar of the Lord

Our high school youth group decided to put on a musical production. Once it had been performed at our home church, leadership decided it would be a good idea to take it on the road to other churches. I was the guy who handled the lights and sound, so of course I had to take everything to the next church and set up the stage accordingly.

At one such church the stage had in its direct center a large, heavy communion table. As there was a fair amount of dance routine in this production, we knew we had to remove that and put it somewhere where it wouldn't interfere. So, I got a group of high school boys together and we proceeded to pick up the communion table and start to move it. Suddenly, an elderly gentleman came puffing up to us yelling, "Stop! Stop!"

He explained, in out-of-breath tones, that we were not to move that table. "That is the altar of the Lord, and it may not be touched by human hands." Which we were okay with, until he told us, "put it back!" Since we had been moving it using human hands there arose the question of how we were to put it back. I solved the problem by making all the boys honorary monkeys. We put it back, and the dancers danced around it all evening.

Moral of the story: Sometimes you need an irreverent way to get around a holy obstacle.

Marriage Encounter

Let me begin this story with a disclaimer: I have no reason to believe that Marriage Encounter is anything but a very helpful ministry, dealing with improving peoples' marriages. We have a couple of friends who were heavily involved in it, and they speak highly of it.

However, I have noticed more than once an interesting and perhaps embarrassing reaction to Marriage Encounter. It goes like this: he's driving the car, she's in the front seat, we are in the backseat. She starts a rant about how terribly difficult it was to drag her husband off to Marriage Encounter. On and on she goes about her difficulties in getting him to agree to go, finally ending with the statement that now he really loves to go. "Don't you, dear?"

Of course, he has been grimacing all through this little tirade and answers that in a very gritted teeth way, "Yes Dear." This has happened with more than one couple, and I wonder: do they really teach the wife to belittle the husband in public like that?

Moral of the story: Don't try to embarrass your spouse into doing something. Speaking privately in the bedroom is greatly preferred to public blackmail.

Hugging

Her name was Cynthia. She was a rather pretty woman, and as most men would put it she was well endowed topside. There are many religious leaders who like to talk about a life changing experience; Cynthia was one of mine.

I grew up in a family where hugging people at random was considered uncouth. You hugged your mother; when you got married you hugged your wife. Anything else was considered out of line. This had to change when we joined a church where people hugged each other all the time. I felt rather embarrassed when they did this and wasn't nearly as warm and responsive as I should've been. Cynthia decided to change that.

I should've mentioned that Cynthia was rather effusive, loud and possessed of a charming smile. She was also a hugger – extraordinaire. One Sunday it started: Cynthia saw me, ran over and gave me a huge hug, squealing "John!!!!!" This soon became her regular habit, which she performed on me two or three times every Sunday. Gradually I got the message that I was going to have to hug back and do so sincerely. My wife and says she never had anything to do with this — but she never objected to it either. I've learned how to hug back and mean it.

Moral of the story: sometimes you ought to try the other person's way of doing it — it might just be better than the way you're doing it now.

Cheerful Giver

John Chrysostom was undoubtedly the greatest preacher the Greek speaking church has ever known. Many things that he has written have impressed me quite a bit, but none more than this. He said that the most important application of the phrase, "God loves a cheerful giver," pertains to the person who is selected to do charitable giving on behalf of the church.

Why? Well, if you're the person running the food pantry or the clothes closet for the church, you're going to meet a lot of people who come in suffering from dire circumstances. A very high proportion of them will be in those circumstances because either they or someone they love did something very stupid. They often show a lack of good sense, and the person on the other side of the counter often concludes that they are in such circumstances because it's their own fault. This tends to provoke people to judge those who are applying for help. The people asking for help are quite sensitive to that attitude, and very often won't ask again if they encounter it. But if that person takes a cheerful attitude, that they just love giving stuff away, those people understand that they are welcome and invited back. So, it is the person who gives on behalf of the church should be the example of cheerful giver.

Moral of the story: Love is given away with a smile and a happy heart. So should clothes and groceries.

Thought Rhymes

One of the most important discoveries I made about the Bible when I was a young man was this: Hebrew poetry really does rhyme. The Psalms really are poems, they rhyme.

At first this seems rather absurd. First, they may rhyme in Hebrew but there's no guarantee they're going to rhyme in English. Well, that depends on what you mean by "rhyme". English poetry rhymes (or at least used to) in sound — rain, plain, Spain, Maine, tune, croon, June, etc. But some poetry rhymes in rhythm — like Japanese haiku, or limericks. Hebrew poetry rhymes in thought. "The Lord is my shepherd" rhymes in thought with "I shall not want."

It can get quite a bit more complicated than that. Psalm 19 starts off with some verses that tell you about how the heat of the sun bakes everything in the desert. It then suddenly switches to the thought, "the law of the Lord is perfect." It's up to you, the reader, to make the connection that says, "you know how the heat of the sun gets into everything in the desert? Same way, the law of the Lord applies to everything." Once I realized this, the Psalms made a lot more sense.

Moral of the story: God is quite unscrupulous in helping you to remember his words. He even uses poetry.

Lower Lights

My uncle Carl owned one of those very elegant looking speedboats with a mahogany deck. It was a boat that had been built in the 1930s; he had lovingly restored it to beautiful condition. One day he took us out on the Ohio River, traveling quite a distance on it to reach a particular restaurant he liked. After dinner, we returned home via the river.

Older Christians will remember the hymn, Let the Lower Lights Be Burning. I saw how it worked that night. Even something as small as a back porch light would cast a glow across the river. This allows you to navigate in the correct channels. A lighthouse would have been blinding but a sixty-watt bulb provides all the light you need.

Moral of the story: The lower lights — that's us — need to be on so that those on the river can find their way home.

World Hunger

One of the difficulties of working in San Francisco is the army of panhandlers and beggars. I took the train to avoid such people. The last few steps to the office led me past one fellow standing there with a sign. He did not speak, and if you looked at his eyes you could tell that his sign was correct; he was blind. He had a bucket for contributions. You could also see that he was suffering from some disease (the sign said AIDS). The sign also said that he was a former Marine and had fought at Da Nang.

I felt rather guilty just walking by him. It nagged me all day the first day I did it. When I got back to my hotel that night and went before God in prayer, I tried to justify my ignoring him. I ended my little speech with the phrase, "after all, I can't solve world hunger."

You don't often hear the voice of God directly — at least I don't. But this night I got it right back. He immediately said to me, "I didn't ask you to solve world hunger. I asked you to feed one of my Marines!" And so I did. There was a fast food joint around the corner and I made it a point every day to see to it that he had a gift certificate that would buy him a decent meal.

Moral of the story: You can't solve world hunger. Feed the hungry you know.

Gold in the Offering Plate

One of the strangest stories I was ever told — and I believe every word of it — came to me from a fellow Christian. He was a member of the Russian Orthodox Church, and in fact was the treasurer for that church in Los Angeles. He told me one day of a puzzle: once a month someone in the congregation — he had no idea who — would place in the offering plate a gold coin, one which came from Russia during the rule of the Czars. I was curious; I asked him if he ever found out to tell me what this was all about.

A few months later I got a call from him. He explained that they had solved the mystery of the gold coins. One of the elderly parishioners had died at home in his small apartment. The landlord of the apartment, knowing that he had no family but the church, asked the church if they would come down and clean out the apartment. The various belongings would be distributed or sold.

As treasurer, he was accustomed to the idea that he would be the man who kept the list of valuables. You can imagine the look on his face when someone first looked under the bed. He found that there were bags, many bags, full of Russian gold coins. Had this fellow taken them down to a coin dealer and sold them, he would've been a rich man. He evidently thought they were worthless because of the communist revolution in Russia.

Moral of the story: That which looks worthless may indeed be golden. Challenge your assumptions.

Marriage

Introduction

"I have done very few smart things in my life," said my father, "but marrying your mother was one of them." I can make a similar statement. More than that, the reason my wife and I have had a relatively calm, loving marriage is greatly attributable to the example my mother and father set. My wife often tells me to this day that she misses my mother, and feels the lack of her good advice and example.

Simply put, I got married and lived happily ever after. Most of the anecdotes you're going to find in this section are of the humorous sort. God has been pleased to bless us both very greatly, and we find our lives together to be so desirable that we have asked God to be kind in making sure neither of us survives the other. As my wife puts it, we want to be "hit by the same meteorite from behind."

So, as you go through this section, laugh at the jokes and learn from the serious stuff.

Encouragement

One of the more memorable things about our engagement was my parents' reaction to it. We came into their bedroom to announce our engagement; they were watching TV while sitting in bed. When we finished our announcement my father got up, put on his bathrobe, shook my hand and congratulated me, and then took my bride to be out to the kitchen for an hour and a half on the subject of why this was a very foolish thing for her to do. At the end of the hour and a half they returned. Mom looked at dad; dad shook his head no; mom got up and put her bathrobe on, did not shake my hand, but did take my bride to be out to the kitchen for another hour of discussion with the same object in mind. Thus began a pattern.

I have never been told that I should not have married Betty. Everyone who has ever made the comparison instantly concludes that I got the better end of the deal. The puzzle is why she married me, not the other way around. I don't know why, but I am exceedingly grateful that she did.

Moral of the story: God is good. Sometimes he blesses you beyond your expectations. When He does, give thanks.

Church on Time

Most people have a little bit of trouble crediting this one, but it is absolutely the fact. My wife was an hour late to our wedding.

I wasn't worried; I had seen her at the church before the ceremony and I knew she was getting ready. I also knew that she is "chronologically challenged," as was the phrase of the day. The minister decided to kick things off after half an hour delay, and the groom and the groomsmen soon were standing at the front. One of those people was Betty's brother, Tom. Very discreetly, he nudged me and pointed at the organist. I was puzzled but he just kept pointing. Then I started to listen to what the organist was playing. I recognized the tune instantly: "Get Me to the Church on Time." The reason it wasn't obvious is that she was playing it in the manner of a Bach fugue. Tom was an excellent musician and he heard it first, but eventually the smiles went around the room.

When I tell this story to friends, I always end it with the same comment: "she was well worth waiting for."

Moral of the story: Wait upon the timing of the Lord. Sometimes He's sharing a laugh with you.

Eyebrow Pencil

Very early in our marriage I encountered a phenomenon which puzzled me. My wife had just left the bathroom when I came into it. I looked down at the toilet and noticed what appeared to be something like wood shavings. One edge of the shavings was dark black; the other edge was blood red.

Now, it was what men generally refer to as "that time of the month." Betty was always pretty good about letting me know when her menstrual period arrived. I searched my memory for what these things could be, and couldn't imagine anything I'd ever heard of before. But looking at them I knew that however she made them in her body, it had to hurt. So, I felt a great deal more sympathy for her — and walked very carefully for the next two or three days.

This went on for fifteen years. Every time I saw that stuff in the toilet, I knew she was in pain and I walked carefully. I still had no idea what it was, but I thought it would be very impolite to ask — so I didn't. One day I walked in on her and found the answer.

She was sharpening her eyebrow pencil over the toilet.

Moral of the story: Sometimes you are not as smart as you think you are.

Valentine's Day

It should be noted that I have never been much of a cook. My wife will allow me to barbecue hamburgers, largely because I've reduced it to the point of a scientific exercise of timing the burgers on each side. Other than that, Betty does the cooking. In this modern, feminist world of ours this may seem a little unusual — but she has a reason.

It stems from Valentine's Day in 1969, just before our wedding. I decided that I was going to host my bride to be in my apartment for a romantic Valentine's Day dinner. Now, it must be remembered that I survived without starving to death solely because there was a supermarket across the street from my apartment building. I went over to the supermarket and purchased a large steak, two baking potatoes, a package of frozen peas, an instant cake mix and an instant frosting mix (just add water.)

When my bride arrived, she discovered that no one had ever told me that baking a potato took longer than broiling a steak. The result was that the steak looked like something that had been through reentry of the atmosphere, while the potatoes had perhaps 1/8 of an inch of a layer of cooked potato on top of the raw. The peas seem to be edible. But it was the cake that convinced her.

Now remember, the cake mix said "just add water." Likewise the frosting mix. They were both designed for an 8 x 8 cake pan, which I had. I had mixed the water with the cake, put it in the cake pan and baked it at the appropriate temperature for the exact time stated on the box. It came out approximately one half of an inch high. The frosting, on the other hand, produced so much that you could have frosted Mount Everest with it.

I decided that something had to be done. So, I went over to the refrigerator to see what I had there that would allow me to improvise. My refrigerator harbored milk, peanut butter, and strawberry jam. I cut the cake diagonally; put it on a plate, added a layer of strawberry jam, put the other half the cake on top and used every bit of frosting on the whole thing. All the great chefs start out with something like this, right?

My bride to be suffered through the steak without complaint; hacked at the potato politely; ate the peas without comment — but the cake was too much. She announced that she would be doing all the cooking in the marriage.

I'd love to tell you that I arranged the whole thing to produce that effect. Honest, I didn't. But just in case you are wondering why Betty does all the cooking...

Moral of the story: If you're going to demonstrate your incompetence, do it with style. Otherwise people might think there's hope for you.

No Man Leaves My House Hungry

One of the things I inherited from my father was this: no man leaves my house hungry. It dates to the days of the Great Depression. Often food was a little short in the house in those days, and even in the better days after I arrived it often happened that expenses were tight. But one thing always prevailed: a guest in our house was well fed. It was my dad's way of teaching me the virtue of hospitality, a neglected virtue in our time.

Moral of the story: Most Christians never achieve greatness. Strive for goodness, even in the small things.

Relocation

For about sixteen years we served with the Lawndale Christian Church. I taught the largest adult Bible Fellowship they had; we had an active ministry. This is the tale of why we left that very good place of service.

I was sitting in my boss's office, shooting the breeze with him. At one point I complained that my commute had greatly lengthened upon moving from the El Segundo office to the Santa Ana office. My boss asked how far, and then reacted with this: "You're entitled to relocation." I told him that no one was going to pay to relocate me from one part of Southern California to another. He proved me wrong; he got the relocation package approved. This confronted me with the question: do you really want to move? You have an active ministry of good service right where you are. I came home that night and told my wife about it. She was quite excited with the thought that we would be moving, and was 100% in favor of leaving. To be specific: "I hate this house, and I hate this neighborhood." That's when I told her I didn't think it was a good idea; this was just God testing us to see if we would hang on in this admittedly rather poor neighborhood. I saw it as a test of whether we would run away from good service merely to have a nicer house and nicer neighborhood.

We argued. We argued for two weeks. At the end of that two weeks I was packing to go on a business trip to Nashville, Tennessee. My wife walked in and announced to me that she had made a decision. She realized we were never going to agree on this. She then stated that I was the husband in the family; I was in charge and we would go with my decision. I would have you note that this was not me convincing her, it was her being obedient to Jesus Christ.

I didn't have a chance to tell my boss I was going to turn it down because I had to go to Nashville. When I got there, I found that the hotel was across the street from the Southern Baptist Bible Bookstore. Imagine your average Bible bookstore; multiply by six — and make it eleven stories high. This Bible teacher was in skunk heaven. I had to carefully plan what I could buy to take back with me because the suitcase would only hold so much.

One of the things that I purchased was a set of tapes (back in those days CDs had yet to come out) of the Gaither Vocal Band. I had one tape, enjoyed the sound but they weren't available locally in California. So, I bought three of their tapes. When I got back to the hotel I started listening to one of the tapes.

About three songs into the tape, the tape player stopped. I looked at the player, but before I could do anything I heard the voice of God: "Listen to the next one. This is for you." That was it. Here are the lyrics from that song:

Beyond the open door lies a new and fresh anointing
Hear the Spirit calling you to go
Walk on through the door, for the Lord will go before you
Into a greater power than you've ever known before

With tears in my eyes, I called Betty and said, "Pack. We're moving." The Lord made good this word for us in the next twenty years in many ways. I don't know what would've happened if Betty had continued to argue, but I know that God honored her obedience by giving us the right answer.

Moral of the story: Don't tell God the solution to the problem; he knows it better than you do. Rather, offer him your obedience and see how he turns it into blessing.

Firm, but Fair

When my two boys were quite young, my wife had a monthly meeting at our church. The custom immediately arose of "Muchachos Night Out." I would take the boys to a local coffee shop; while we were there, they got to play with some toys that were specifically reserved for restaurants. This one particular evening they were exceptionally well behaved — something I didn't notice until it was pointed out to me.

The man at the next table was wearing enough "bling" to sink a small battleship. He was about 50 or so, and was obviously courting the sweet young thing opposite him at the table. She was much younger than he was. I noticed that he kept looking over at our table, rather nervously. As I had not seen him before I was a little puzzled by this. Finally, he and his date got up to leave — but before he did he came over to our table and asked me, "how do you do it?" "How do I do what?" He explained that he had raised children of his own and that when they went out to restaurants they were ill behaved little brats. He wanted to know how I had managed to train mine so that they behaved so well. I didn't have the heart to tell them that this was a random coincidence; usually at least one child could be counted on to raise a fuss. So I told him, simply, "you have to be firm but fair with them." He nodded as if he was a man enlightened by some Himalayan Guru. With an admirable bit of self-control, I restrained myself from laughing out loud until he and his date were gone.

Moral of the story: If everything goes well, take credit for it.

Blonde in Montreal

One of the more interesting experiences in my life came when I wrote a small piece of software for the computers that my company made. It had a usefulness well beyond my own, and on the strength of that I was invited to the annual customer conference. It was being held in Montréal that year and like most such it was a very festive conference. We entertained our customers there; it was mostly a marketing occasion.

Besides myself, six other people from our department were invited, all technical experts. These were people I lived with day by day. One of the interesting things about this group of people was that they held a very different view of sexual relations than I do. They believed in casual sex; sex with anybody, as long as it was consenting, was a great idea. Just to state the obvious: I believe that sex occurs with your wife, and nobody else, starting on your wedding night.

The second night we were there the seven of us were seated at a table with one stranger. The stranger was a very good-looking blonde and she had been seated next to me. When the after dinner conversation began, she came right to the point. "I want to make love with you tonight." Please note, I had never seen this woman before that night. I explained that I didn't do that. As I did so, I noticed that all conversation had ceased and all six of the other people were watching me. We went through arguments like, "You like steak, why not try chicken?" But it boiled down to the fact that, even though we were in Montréal, I would still know about my adultery. I told the lady that marriage was about honesty more than sex, and I had given my wife my word I would not do such a thing. After a good deal of persistence, she finally gave up. I was polite all through the discussion, thinking that she was a customer. But it occurred to me later that my coworkers may have arranged this. It would be easy enough to find a cute prostitute and see whether this man really meant what he said. I noticed a change in attitude after that. To this day, I'm still curious as to where she came from.

Moral of the story: Getting out of town is not the same as getting out of a commitment. Sex when out of town and "it's okay as long as my wife doesn't know" is rightly judged to be hypocrisy.

Redhead in Cleveland

The corporate headquarters of my company in this job was in Cleveland. One of the geniuses there had invented what he thought was going to be a world beating program for doing spreadsheets. This was in the days before Microsoft was doing this type of software, and as the junior programmer I was sent to the class to learn how to use the product — and to decide on whether we were going to purchase it.

The travel schedule was somewhat unusual. I was told that I had to be at a meeting at noon on Sunday before the class. This was unique in my experience. When I got there, the party was in full swing. It was a luncheon meeting, and nobody discussed business. Seated next to me was a gorgeous redhead who seemed to pay quite a bit of attention to everything I said.

This would've passed off as just something a little odd except for the fact that every night of the class we all went out to dinner together — required. That same redhead, who was not in the class (she was a keypunch operator), was seated next to me at each of these meals. On Thursday night, the last night we would meet together, she offered to take me back to my hotel. I accepted, and she followed me into the lobby. She then asked me whether I would like to have her come up to my room. I said I thought that would be most inappropriate.

Her reaction stunned me. She burst into tears. When I managed to get her calmed down she explained why she was there at all. It seems that the guy who produced this software had noticed that the commercial applications on the market were quite a bit better than his product. So, he forced some of the girls in the keypunch room to join us for meals — and to make sure that they seduced us while we were in Cleveland. This would provide adequate blackmail to ensure that we would recommend his product when we returned to our individual units. She was told that if she didn't seduce me she would be fired. As she was a single mother with two children, this would have been devastating. I was absolutely flabbergasted that anybody would do a thing like this.

When I got back I discussed it with my boss and basically got two decisions. One was that I was obviously being a little naïve about this; this sort of thing happened all the time. The second was that there was nothing we, in our subordinate position, could do about it. As it happens, the individual who did this was asked to leave the company about six months later for some other reason.

Of course, today, something like this would be meat and potatoes for some lawyer. But in the bad old days all we could do was sit down and shut up.

Moral of the story: There are wicked people out there. Just when you're thinking, "nobody would do that" somebody does.

Chuck E. Cheese's

One of the couples in our Bible class at Lawndale Christian Church adopted a set of twin children. Their biological mother had been drug addicted, and of course this affected their behavior quite a bit. "Rambunctious" was often a mild description of their behavior.

As the time came up for them to finalize the adoption, they asked if I would like to be one of the witnesses who would sign the documents. It's somewhat of a formal ceremony. I said I would be delighted to do so.

It turns out that the judge presiding over this ceremony was Lance Ito, the judge in the O. J. Simpson case, but before that case came out. I distinctly remember the end of the ceremony. We had gotten to the point where one last signature was required, and the adoption would be official. Judge Ito leaned over his desk and asked one of the twins, Robbie, "do you know what this means?"

Robbie gave him a look that kids have when adults ask them a really stupid question. "Sure! It means we get to go to Chuck E. Cheese's!"

Moral of the story: Sometimes things look different from a lower altitude.

Hey Babe!!

One of the ways your wife teaches you that she is not just a sex object — is to be one heck of a sex object. That doesn't make much sense right now, but bear with me, it will.

I was watching a football game on our 9-inch diagonal screen black and white TV, early in our marriage. My wife had been kind enough to bring me a bowl of potato chips and a beer to accompany the game. Time went on, the chips disappeared, and the beer was gone. So, as halftime approached, I saw her going by on some errands and I said, "Hey babe! Another beer and more chips!"

She smiled, and said nothing. I dismissed it from my mind as a little joke between the two of us - until she came back with another beer and some more chips. That was not the astonishing part. She was wearing the highest heels she had, fishnet pantyhose and a leopard print micro mini dress not suitable for wear in public. She was wearing nothing else — I checked. Carefully. Very carefully.

Somehow, I lost interest in the football game, and as you can imagine we spent the afternoon in the bedroom. But the incident had its lasting effects. Every time I started to complain about how my wife just didn't want to have sex often enough with me, she would smile and ask if I'd like to see her in the leopard print dress again. The answer was always yes, but it served as a reminder that she was perfectly willing to be a sex object for me; perhaps it was my desire to have a sex object constantly at my beck and call that was the problem.

Note please she could've argued with me about it. She didn't. She gave me what I wanted, and used it as a reminder that it wasn't her willingness to play that was the problem.

Moral of the story: Your wife is not a toy. Curb your desires, and treat her with respect.

School

Introduction

School has been an important part of my life. I have a Masters in physics, and an MBA, so I'm not particularly inexperienced at it. I started out to be a high school physics teacher; my service in the Army prevented me from being hired. But in the time I spent in school, as student or teacher, some interesting things happened. Some of them are rather serious; some are rather humorous. Enjoy.

Memorable Teachers

Over the years I have had many teachers. But in the first 12 years of my education very few stood out in one way or another. Here are three that did.

- *Dr. Lorens* - he was the best elementary school teacher I ever had. He had worked as a professor in the Department of Education at a major university until they forcibly retired him. He then picked a school district in which he taught fifth grade. He taught me how to speed read (invaluable in college). He took me and a couple of the other boys on a tour of Los Angeles harbor, an introduction into the adult world. He taught me all sorts of mathematics tricks. But mostly, he showed me that he cared about those in the classroom who were different.
- *Mr. Steinkraus* - he was my favorite math teacher in high school. I've never met a teacher who so instinctively knew how to motivate students. Interestingly, when my sister had him as a math teacher she absolutely hated him — because he said that he believed that girls just couldn't do math. This may have had something to do with her going on to be a math major in college and then become a math teacher.
- *Miss Hornbuckle* – everyone has somebody like her as a teacher at one time or another. She could walk through a mob of riot crazed aborigines and strike fear in every heart. She was well over 9000 years old when I met her, and every student at Rancier Junior High went about in complete terror of her. She had a steel I-beam where most people have a backbone. Rumor had it that she could just look at a planet and stop it in mid-orbit. But what she taught you about English, you remembered.

59

Widget

One of the less pleasing classes I had to take when I got my MBA was International Business. The instructor was a French war bride (divorced), card-carrying communist who generally despised Americans whom she considered to be totally ignorant of anything really important. We looked for good ways to get back at her, and one night we had a dandy.

The textbook we used often referenced the word "widget" in the usual meaning of a technical device not specified. There really is no such thing as a widget, but it represents some device whose name you don't know yet. Our instructor, however, had not gathered this point. So, about 10 minutes before class started she asked me, "what is this widget the book keeps talking about?" Have you ever had one of those situations where you knew there was the exact right thing to say, if you could just think of it in time? This time, I thought of it in time. I calmly replied, "analog or digital?"

I wasn't exactly sure where I was going to go with that discussion, but I was sure it was going to lead someplace humorous. What took place next, though, changed the whole discussion completely. A buddy of mine was sitting at a desk across the room and joined the conversation this way: he slammed his fist down on the desk and yelled at the top of his lungs, "THE DIGITAL WIDGET IS THE WAVE OF THE FUTURE!" And the argument was on! He and I argued in technical terms about whether the widget of whatever type would work for whatever application. One of his friends on the other side of the room slipped out and told the people coming into class what was going on. Pretty soon the guys in the banking business were talking vigorously about whether they would loan money to a firm that was making digital widgets. All sorts of financial numbers went around the room, all sorts of engineering concepts went around the room until we had constructed an absolutely bewildering array of arguments for and against the digital widget. 20 minutes into the class time she finally got wise that she'd better start talking herself. She never did get an explanation of the widget.

Moral of the story: There is no target so attractive as someone who is sneering at you.

Ignorant Individuals

One of the most common experiences in college is to encounter a professor who is determined to shrink the number of people taking his class. This may be sheer laziness on his part, or maybe he thinks he's guarding the precious entrance to the portals of knowledge, or whatever — but the technique is pretty standard. Here's how it went in an art class that I took when I was a senior at UCLA.

The instructor walked in, and the first thing you noticed was that he was the spitting image of Gen. Burkhalter on the program Hogan's Heroes. He had the same accent too. So, when he got to the podium, 300 people, mostly freshman, were treated to this opening monologue.

"Most of you here are products of the American educational system. I like that. Because the American system produces individuals. Not like the German system; the German system produces masses. But the American system produces individuals. IGNORANT INDIVIDUALS!"

(You must hear that one with him speaking with the German accent; if you're a freshman it was really scary). As I was a senior at the time; I just chuckled, but you could see the look of panic on a lot of the freshman faces.

Moral of the story: Sometimes experience is the best guardian against fraud.

When You Get the Only "A"

This little incident happened to me at Loyola Marymount University, while I was getting my MBA. One of the required courses was Business Law. Our instructor was a practicing attorney who opened the class by announcing that as there were ten of us in the class, he would give one A, two B's, three C's and four D's. As this was a graduate course, and very often the first course people took in the MBA program, we assumed that he was kidding. If he did that seven out of the ten people in the class would be either on academic probation or gone from the program.

The course worked its way through to the end; we took the final exam and received those little postcards we had in those days to tell us what our grade was. I received the only "A". A few phone calls confirmed the fact that he had not been kidding about that distribution of grades. This seemed grossly unfair to me, because all ten of the people in question evidenced that they had learned the material quite well.

So, I went to the Dean. I walked into his office, explained which course I was talking about, and showed him my grade card and told him that I was apparently the only person to get an "A". I explained that I thought this was unfair, unjust and was liable to cost the program some very good people. The Dean said he would look into the matter.

He did, and the grading structure was altered. We never saw that instructor again either. The point I would make is this: if you get the only "A", you have the obligation of taking the issue up with whoever is in authority. Someone who gets a "D" is complaining; the person who gets the "A" is trying to fix the problem.

Moral of the story: You may not be the cause of injustice - but you might be the solution. Imitate God - do justice.

Elementary, Einstein

It's very impressive to some people to say that you have a Master's degree in physics. It's not so impressive to tell them how you struggled with that, and that you simply got through the program more than anything else. However, occasionally you might show flashes of something that might be described as sheer brilliance — or hilarious good luck.

It happened this way. I was taking a course in Einstein's General Theory of Relativity — and it is every bit as hard as you can imagine it to be. It was made worse by the fact that the instructor spoke with a thick Czechoslovakian accent of some sort. Some of us actually thought they should send in a translator. So, I followed my usual rule on this: take good notes, keep your head down and never ask questions. If you ask no questions, the instructor can't confirm the fact that you really don't belong there.

This was the last semester of my Master's program. To get the degree I had to pass a series of oral exams on practically every subject in physics. I was fortunate enough to be one of only 2 candidates being examined that semester; the other fella had been out of studies for a year and had just flown in from Philadelphia. It turned out that he was even more ignorant than I was, and the board just did not have the heart to turn the man down. Logically, of course, if they passed him they had to pass me — and they did.

One of my fellow teaching assistants there, a magnificent Swede from Minnesota named Swenson, offered to "buy me a beer." Beware of Swedes from Minnesota mentioning "a beer." He took me over to the local tavern and we proceeded to have beer. People would come in — this place was a favorite of the department — and Swenson would yell, "hey, Hendershot just passed his orals!" The person would usually reply, "great, I'll buy you a beer." When we had done this long enough that reality had faded completely from existence, Swenson sat straight up and said, "we have to go to class now." We drove across the street to get to that Relativity class.

Now, my usual method was not going to work that night. I was in no shape whatsoever to take notes, and I was a little leery of putting my head down looking like I was doing it. So, I watched the instructor. Five minutes into the class, I did something I never had done before: I asked a question.

About 45 minutes later I sobered up enough to realize two things: first, the professor was sweating blood trying to answer my question. He was obviously deeply impressed by the brilliance that I had displayed. Second, to this day I have no idea what the question was. The absurdity was made complete when at the end of class, the boy genius — a junior in physics, but taking this graduate course — came up to me and asked, "how did you ever think of that?" I replied, "it's an elementary consequence of the equivalence principle. Think about it." (If you know something about it, you know this is a rather sneering reply.)

But it did pay off for me. When we got to the final exam I knew there was going be one question that started with about 4 or 5 lines of mathematics, then proceeded into the proof of a theorem, and then another couple lines of math that demonstrate the answer. It's one of those problems it takes half an hour to an hour to solve — and when I got to the final I didn't have that much time. So, I wrote down the first 5 lines, then I put down "it is obvious that..." and then the theorem I was supposed to prove, followed by the last little bit of math. I got an A in the course. Ever since then I've always wondered whether Einstein thought up his theory when he was drunk.

Moral of the story: When brains fail you, try hard work. If that doesn't do it, count on dumb luck.

Dad Knew My Name

One of the common problems of the military family is that the children rarely get to spend more than one year in the same school. School administrators don't like this; it disrupts the routine. One day I disrupted it a whole lot more than usual.

The teacher was taking roll. When she got to my name, she said "Henderson?"

I replied, as politely as a third grader could, that my name was Hendershot. She replied politely, "young man, don't you play tricks on me."

You can leave the rest of the argument right there; she just wasn't going to believe my last name. Eventually we got to the point of "you're going to the principal's office unless you behave" which was responded to with a "go ahead, I know my own name."

So, off to the principal's office I go. He, per procedure, called my father to come pick me up. Dad showed up in full military dress uniform, which includes a name tag. He was armed with a 45 automatic. The principal got into his unctuous little speech about 8 or 9 sentences worth when he spotted the name tag, and stopped.

My father turned to me, and in an exquisite phrase said, "young man, you have permission to wait outside the office." Dad was very insistent that we were not to use military language. He, however, was an absolute master of it. He also had a great deal of experience in the art of chewing someone's rear end. The principal got the very best of everything he had learned. I never went back to that 3rd grade class; they tested me and decided I needed to skip to the 4th grade. All things considered, if I knew then what I know now about it I would've refused to skip. But I know that teacher never wanted to see me in her classroom again.

Moral of the story: When you know you're right, persist.

Sadie Hawkins Dance

When I had reached the ripe old age of 13 or so, one of the young ladies in my class invited me to escort her to the school's annual Sadie Hawkins dance. If you're not familiar with the custom, at a Sadie Hawkins dance the girl invites the boy. At that time women's liberation had not proceeded beyond that point. Socially speaking, it is considered bad style for the male to refuse the invitation. So my mother informed me, so therefore I accepted — knowing full well I could not dance a step.

I thought about declining it, but my father insisted that the young gentleman at some time or other had to learn how to dance. Knowing full well that Fred Astaire was not trembling in his shoes, he sent me off to the local dance Academy.

My status as a complete klutz was brought forward in my effort to dance. This was one of those studios that thought they could teach anybody. They assigned me a female partner, one who was the daughter of the owner of the dance studio. Her name was Ann Lusty, believe it or not. Even worse, she was a gorgeous blonde about a year older than myself. As you can imagine she danced quite well. Unfortunately, she was subjected to the torture of having to dance with me, which is something like dancing with a drunken elephant. I eventually got out of the dance class, into the Sadie Hawkins dance and spent most of it standing around the tables where they had the red punch. But even after all these years, I think I owe Ann an apology (or several). I never did learn how to dance.

Moral of the story: No matter how much you know about math and physics, if you're a klutz, you're a klutz.

What a Hit

My grandfather was a pitcher in the major leagues for some years. I suspect my father inherited some of his talent, but by the time it reached my generation it was completely gone. This was exemplified one day in an intramural baseball game at UCLA.

We were in one of those facilities where there are no fences defining the field. There were no bleachers or seats either, so both teams just sort of stood around on one side or the other. When it was my turn to bat, I walked up to the plate and poked at two pitches. The next pitch coming down, though, was an absolute gem for a hitter. It was belt high, right across the middle of the plate. I got every little bit of it; the ball took off like a rocket.

As I was rounding first base, I could hear our guys chanting: "What a Hit! What a Hit! What a Hit!" I had a smile that would've lit up Los Angeles, and it only got bigger as I rounded second base. But as I headed towards third base I heard the other team chanting: "What a Catch! What a Catch! What a Catch!" I love baseball particularly, most sports in general, but my playing career can be summed up in one word: "almost."

Moral of the story: No matter what inflates your ego or how fast it does it, there's somebody around with a pin to poke it.

Teaching Astronomy

In my college career, I started out to become a high school physics teacher. I love physics, and I knew I wasn't Albert Einstein, so I figured high school physics I could do. By a wonderful coincidence of circumstances, I was offered a job at Beverly Hills High School. My day consisted of three classes in general science and two teaching astronomy.

One day my master teacher, the department chairman, pointed out one of my astronomy students and asked me, "do you know who that is?" Being new at this I assumed he wanted to know whether or not I had memorized my students' names, so I said, "of course. That's Carrie."

"No — I mean do you know who that IS?" I replied with a puzzled look, not really understanding the question. It seems that, at this school, spotting the children of movie stars is sort of a pleasant game. He told me, "that's Debbie Reynold's daughter." The name would've meant nothing to me at the time, and it was a good number of years later when I remembered that her father was the singer, Eddie Fisher. And by now I think you've guessed it, this is the Carrie Fisher who played Princess Leia in Star Wars. That's right, I'm the guy who taught astronomy to Princess Leia.

(I strongly suspect she would not know my name after leaving the class. Maybe it's just my "close to famous" moment.)

Moral of the story: Pretty much everyone has an odd coincidence, a "next door to famous" experience. They are fun to tell, and I thank you for listening to mine.

Nobel Prize

Most teachers will tell you that, after a few years, they forget most of their students' names. I will never forget Barry's name.

Barry was one of my physics students. It was a Tuesday-Thursday class, and very often on Tuesday Barry would open the class by raising his hand. He would start with something like this: "Mr. Hendershot, I've been thinking about what you said last Thursday, and I have a question."

The questions Barry asked were invariably deep and profound questions about physics. I often found myself saying, "Barry, I'll have to get back to you on that." Barry was obviously head and shoulders above anybody else I had ever seen in physics when it came to that natural understanding of pure genius level physics.

So, as the semester ended, I took Barry aside and endeavored to persuade him to be a physics major in college. It was a very frustrating experience for me. He wanted to be a doctor, like his father, and didn't really think physics held any attraction to him. I got to the point of telling him, "Barry, your Nobel Prize is waiting for you." He replied with something like, "no, I just want to go to medical school like my dad."

It wasn't until the end of the semester that I was let in on the joke. Those questions weren't from Barry at all. He was going over to his next-door neighbor and getting some coaching. His next-door neighbor was Richard Feynman, who in 1965 did win the Nobel Prize in physics.

Moral of the story: Try not to take reality at face value — it may be lying to you.

Drug-Crazed Baby Killer

You might be wondering at this point why I never went back to teaching. After all, I had a job at one of the best schools in the state. I also had a commitment to the U.S. Army.

The reason I never went back to teaching is best exemplified by the Long Beach City Schools. I had an appointment to interview for a job as a physics teacher. I never actually got to the appointment. The clerk behind the counter called me up and told me there had been a mistake in reading my resumé; they thought I was a civilian at Fort Ord. I began to politely explain that this was incorrect and that my resumé certainly did make this clear. I never finished my sentence.

The clerk tore my resumé up, threw it in my face, and yelled "Get out of here! We don't want any drug-crazed baby killers teaching our children!" (The room broke into applause.) I found that having been in the Army was quite sufficient to prevent me from even getting an interview at any other school, except one. That school ended the interview with the phrase, "We were hoping that you were black."

Moral of the story: Sometimes God has other plans for what he wants you to do. Do the best you can with what he gives you; He knows what he's doing.

Eye Patch

Introduction

With my sincere thanks to Robert Louis Stevenson (Treasure Island) and to J. M. Barrie (Peter Pan) I have a predefined role I am obliged to play: Pirate. My grandchildren know me as "Grandpa Pirate". Over the years I have discovered that some children are afraid of pirates, while most kids think it's delightful to have one around. You get used to answering the same questions about your eyepatch and as you will see there are some themes that come out when you live the life of a pirate with an eyepatch.

All in all, I've had a lot of fun with it. It's very rare that I actually frighten someone, at least among the children. So, enjoy the stories of what it's like to be both a grandfather and a pirate.

You Go Ask Him

It is practically a mathematical certainty: if a 5-year-old sees you with an eye patch, you are without doubt a pirate.

One Sunday afternoon my wife and I took in a concert at the Richard Nixon Library. I was dressed in a white turtleneck with my black sports jacket, which is probably as close as I get to being a pirate in apparel. We stopped at the supermarket on the way home. As we were checking out, about 2 aisles over there was a young lady with a 5-year-old. Taking a good look at me, he looked up at her and said (in a stage whisper you could hear all over the store), "Mom! A pirate! A real pirate!"

Everyone at the checkstands tried to find a way to muffle the laughter. My wife struck up a friendly conversation with the woman, and explained that not only was I happy to be a pirate but I make balloon animals for young kids. She invited the lady to bring the kid over, but before she could do so the kid piped up, "mom — is he a real pirate?"

In the sweetest voice you can imagine, his mother said: "why don't you go over and ask him, dear?"

"No! YOU go ask him." We never did get him to come over any closer.

Moral of the story: If life hands you an eyepatch, enjoy being the pirate.

Popeye, the Ironworker

One of the disadvantages of wearing a pirate's eyepatch — and I wear it for medical reasons, not as a fashion statement — is that some men view it as a challenge. This one I remember quite well. It started with the two of us coming around the corner of the aisles in the supermarket; we were about 2 aisles apart. If you can imagine Popeye the sailor with a goatee, you have a very good picture of him. His forearms were thicker than my thighs. He looked up and saw me and reacted with a jolt. If you could read his mind from what was on his face, he was thinking "I wonder if that guy is as tough as I am."

If you could have read my facial expression, you would've gotten "oh Lord, don't let him find out."

It turns out that he was an ironworker, a guy who carried steel I-beams around. Like me, he was pushing the cart for his wife, so all passed off without any violence. But you gotta be careful sometimes.

Moral of the story: Being easily misunderstood is not protection against getting clobbered.

Balloon Animals

I'm sure it's rather unusual, but I always carry a few balloons and a pump to make balloon animals. It's a result of the eyepatch, really. Most children react to it in a positive way. They can be curious, they can be excited that they found a real pirate, they can look at you and ask what's wrong with your eye. But the one thing you don't want them to do is to react as if they're frightened out of their wits.

To counter this, I carry those balloon animals. When somebody is screeching I walk over, pull out the pump and the balloon, and ask the kid if he likes balloons. If he says yes, I ask if he likes animals. If he says yes, then I tell him he obviously would like to have a balloon animal. I then make one for him. By the time I get done he has been completely distracted from his terror.

There is a dark side to this. Sometimes you encounter a kid who is scared because his life is scary. You have the feeling that something was wrong in that home, and balloon animals won't fix it.

Moral of the story: Sometimes a balloon animal is more than just hot air under pressure.

Captain Hook

For most children the knowledge of an eyepatch being connected with a pirate starts at around four years old. Children younger than that usually are curious about the patch, but they don't associate it with being a pirate. Some children, however, have a bit more of an advantage at home. We found this out one night at a restaurant at which a young lady was picking up a "to go" order. She had her 18 month old son with her. He took one look at me, ran around the other side of mom holding on for dear life. He looked up at her and said, "Captain Hook!"

I was going to say, "Thank you very much, Walt Disney" (assuming that's where he first saw Captain Hook) but then I recalled that Disney's Captain Hook doesn't wear an eyepatch. You figure it out.

Moral of the story: Sometimes you are a pirate despite wearing an eyepatch.

Other

Introduction

The stories in this section just don't fit anywhere else. They tend to be a rather serious bunch of things, too. The story about the Liberty Bell stirs deep emotions in me; prison ministry has long been a part of our life. Some of these stories, like the one about the prisoners being allowed to say they've never been arrested before, taught me a lot. I suggest you read them one at a time as they are not particularly related to each other.

Liberty Bell

Humidity was invented in Philadelphia -- probably by Benjamin Franklin. It was that kind of a day. My wife and I, with our two boys (our daughter not yet born) were visiting my sister and her family in New Jersey. We took some time to visit the city of Philadelphia, in particular Independence Hall.

Independence Hall is the place where the Declaration of Independence was signed. As we entered the hall, our families split up into small groups. I had only my two boys with me when we went into the small outdoor pavilion in which the Liberty Bell is kept.

Our tour guide must have been affected by the humidity. She was a summer hire, and obviously tired and bored. In a sing-song voice that matched the weather, she told us about the bell: where it was cast; how much it weighed; how it was brought to Philadelphia; for whom it was tolling when it cracked -- I've forgotten everything she said that day.

Except for the last two sentences: *"If you are an American citizen, the Liberty Bell is part of your heritage. You are permitted to touch the Bell."*

Touch the Liberty Bell? You might as well have told me that I could take home the original Declaration of Independence. My father raised his son a patriot. I get a lump in my throat when the flag is paraded by; I can't finish the Star-Spangled Banner at ball games (and not just because of the high notes). The thought of touching the Liberty Bell stirred deep emotions within me.

We waited until all the others in our group had filed out. I took my sons forward. I told my oldest boy to touch the Bell. He did so, with all the solemn dignity that only a five year old can have when doing a very "adult" thing.

I picked up my two-year-old son, and told him to touch the Bell. He pounded on it with both hands, as a toddler will, with a big smile on his face. Is there any joy like that of a toddler having fun in his father's arms?

When I put him down, I took a moment to reflect. Then, eyes wet, with my own two hands, I reached out and touched the Liberty Bell.

If you are not a patriot, I cannot explain the moment. If you are a patriot, I need not.

Moral of the story: You have been blessed by Almighty God with the privilege of being born a citizen of the greatest nation He has ever permitted. Know it, experience it and thank God for it.

Meaning of the Word

As any parent will tell you, there occasionally comes a moment when your kid shows far more perception than you ever thought possible. My oldest boy was about three years old. We were teaching him to use the words "please" and "thank you" so as to ask politely for things. The other big emphasis in it in his life was that he is to share his toys with the other kids in the neighborhood. He was, at that time, an only child so we put some emphasis on that.

One of the ways we taught him to ask politely was that when dad was having a beer and watching a `1`baseball game, he could get a ladle full of beer by saying please and thank you. Motivation, you see. One day we got a different method. He came in, saw that I was drinking a beer and watching a ballgame, and went over into a corner to play with his toys. When I had dismissed all thought of the ladle full of beer, he came up to me with this approach.

"Daddy, you know the meaning of lots of words, don't you daddy?"

"Yes Doug, daddy knows the meaning of lots of words."

"Daddy you know the meaning of every word there is, don't you daddy?"

At this point I was wondering what set of obscenities he might've picked up from someplace else, and was a little apprehensive that I might have to explain something that he shouldn't use. So, I kind of hedged a little bit.

"Well Doug, daddy knows the meaning of lots of words."

"Then you know the meaning of the word 'share', don't you daddy?"

He got his beer.

Moral of the story: You teach your kids their lessons, they teach them back to you.

Picked Enough

Many years ago, when I was a young boy, I lived in paradise. When your father is a soldier, living on a proving ground is paradise. Airplanes, tanks, artillery, helicopters were an everyday sight to me.

The government obtained Jefferson Proving Ground by buying a large chunk of Southern Indiana, fencing it off, and firing artillery into it. The farms and such were left as they were, and many things grew wild there. Including blackberries.

My uncle and his family came down from Ohio to visit us. My father instructed them all on the dangers of artillery rounds not yet exploded – the base was very strict about this; these things are dangerous – but his instruction was met with a pleasant smile. No one was concerned.

We went out to pick blackberries. Have you ever been in a blackberry bramble? Then you know that it doesn't move very quickly. But this day it parted – like the Red Sea for Moses. My uncle let out a yell and began running back down the road.

We ran with him. One of the things you learn on a proving ground is to run when the other guy does – you can always ask questions later. But when we were out of breath, all we could get out of him was a dignified, "I think we've picked enough today."

That's a perfectly natural reaction for a man who has just kicked a sixteen inch (diameter), 2700-pound artillery shell.

Moral of the story: Sometimes the sky is falling. Keep your eyes open.

Diamond in the Sink

My wife is not a woman given to "water power." She does not go into tears over the minor upsets of life. She is not one of those women who use tears as a weapon to get what she wants. When she cries, she means it. When she cries, I pay attention.

So, you can imagine that I was extremely concerned when I came home one day to find her hovering over our kitchen sink, bawling her eyes out. She was clearly crying over something in the sink, and it wasn't onions. It took some time for me to get her sufficiently calmed to find out what happened.

She was crying because she had lost the diamond out of her engagement ring. It's interesting to see the difference in our reactions. My first thought was, "You've got to be kidding?" (If you knew how little that diamond cost -- and it was the biggest one I could afford at the time -- you'd understand my first reaction). To me, it was a relatively inexpensive gemstone.

To her, however, it represented her marriage. She had lost the symbol of something which (she tells me) makes her happy. I began to think about it in a different light.

Isn't it interesting that the deepest form of communication in our species is symbolic communication? It is the least precise form of communication, to be sure, because its meaning depends both on the one talking and the one listening. For example, when I see an American flag -- a symbol -- it carries deep meaning to me. For many people it does also, but the meaning is somewhat different. Yet we refer to these meanings by the same symbol. The communication is not complete in what I say when I show the flag; it needs your experience to be complete communication. To my wife, that ring was symbolic communication from me to her, and it was very precious.

That's symbolic communication. It needs a symbol, like the engagement ring. It needs a sender, but it is not complete without the experience of the receiver. The deeper the experience on both sides, the more meaningful the communication.

Moral of the story: It's never "just a symbol." The cross, the flag, your wedding ring are much more than the material they are made from.

The Milkman

In every junior high school class, there is a goddess. She's the girl who has the perfect face and the perfect figure — and who does not date dorks, but only football players. She knows she can get any guy she wants with a smile, and is very discriminating about who she gets.

In my junior high school class, this young lady was a member of the youth group at my church. Perhaps more importantly, her mother was in the same Bible class that my mom was in. One Sunday, my mother promised this lady she would send her a copy of a cookie recipe. The next Saturday, I was duly tasked with getting on my bike and riding over to deliver the recipe. I was hoping that mom would be home, and I wouldn't have to face the goddess. (Actually, she was pretty nice.)

I got there and rang the doorbell. I could hear somebody scurrying down the stairs, the door being unlocked and opened. The door opened, and there was the goddess. Except for a towel around her head, she was absolutely stark naked.

Full. Frontal. Nudity.

This is not something that happens within the ordinary experience of a Christian gentleman, let alone an eighth grade kid. I stood there dumbfounded and waited for her to say something. What she said seemed to me to be crazy: "oh! I thought you were the milkman."

I handed her the recipe, told her to give it to her mother, and closed the door. Then I went home to see if I could find some eyeball bleach.

It isn't as crazy as it seems. In those days a milkman would deliver milk to your front door. The custom was that he would ring the doorbell to let you know he had arrived, but would not stay to chat. So, he would deposit the milk, ring the doorbell, and leave as quickly as possible.

Moral of the story: Just because you have a plan to handle all possible situations doesn't mean that life won't give you an impossible situation.

Prison Ministry

It is a fact: the typical, middle-class Christian wants absolutely nothing to do with prison ministry. They see it as something to be done by someone's Rescue Ministry. We can certainly understand that feeling; here's how my wife reacted to the first time she visited someone in prison.

One of the students in my Bible class, Donnie, was arrested and convicted for some very serious crimes and sent to a prison in central California. We took a weekend off, and as part of our vacation we visited Donnie at the prison. This wasn't behind the walls; it was in the visitor room. When we left my wife was unusually silent.

We went through a series of doors clanging — do you remember the opening sequence for Maxwell Smart? All those prison doors clanging behind him? That's what it sounded like. My wife said not a word. We went outside and got in the car, and it was not until we were back on the main highway, completely off the prison grounds, that she spoke.

"I want to go back to the motel, take my clothes off and burn them, and then take a shower with Fel's Naphtha soap and a brush."

That is how it felt for her. It's a natural reaction to the environment. But as we got more experienced at it, it was less and less a problem. Later, we had the opportunity to work with Bill Glass Behind the Walls and go into the prison yard itself. It sounds more dangerous, but it really isn't. The glory of it is that prisoners are people who know they are sinners, know they need a Savior — and are grateful when you introduce him. Results vary; I had weekends where no one accepted Christ listening to me. I've also had weekends where as many as nine prisoners accepted Christ as their Savior. You may think this is dirty work; it is also work that is very profitable for the kingdom of God.

Moral of the story: In working for the Kingdom, take the opportunities that God gives you. Little is much when God is in it.

You May Now Say

Prison ministry includes visits to the courtroom as well as visits to the prison. We were walking alongside one of our Bible class members during his trial. The way these things work: you show up at 9 o'clock, and then sometime that same day the judge will take up the case you're interested in. So of course, we were there a little early.

As we came in I noticed several chairs lined up on one of the walls. People were coming in and selecting a particular chair. I didn't know it at the time, but they were in alphabetical order. The judge came in a little later, with a huge stack of dark manila folders. The first item of business he came to was dealing with all these people sitting in those chairs.

He would call the man forward. He then opened his manila folder and mumbled things like, "I see you have completed the required training. I see you have been sober for 3 years." But he always ended with, "you may now say that you have never been arrested for drunk driving."

My first reaction to this was "what you mean you can say that? Why the heck are you here if not for drunk driving?" But as I thought about it, I realized that this was the judicial system's way of granting forgiveness. Most of these people were Hispanic, economically lower-class. With a conviction for drunk driving, they weren't likely to get a job at all, particularly one that required a driver's license. So, this method let them back into the labor market, and since most of them looked old enough to have a family to support it was probably a good thing.

It makes you think. How many times have you been told that people advance until they make their first mistake? When it comes to judging others, we expect perfection from everyone but ourselves.

Moral of the story: Always find a way to forgive. You never know when you might need it yourself.

Heart Attack

A heart attack can be an educational experience — if you survive it.

I had one while I was on assignment to put in some systems in the Napa Valley. It started with pain in the chest which I attributed to heartburn. I began to take various forms of antacids and by 6 o'clock in the morning I concluded that this was not working. One of the companies for whom I had worked taught us that in these circumstances you want to call the front desk and have them call 911. That way, the fire department can find room 246 without any trouble.

Before I left for the hospital I was able to talk to my wife and tell her what was going on, and of course I told her not to worry. Which of course I knew was not going to be of any effect whatsoever. What's interesting to me is the reaction of other people around.

Let's start with the crew of technicians I had working with me. They obviously missed my presence at the jobsite that morning, and one of them had the presence of mind to call the hospital (it was the only one in the Valley) and ask if I was there. Bingo! So, the entire crew of them came over to visit me. My lead technician informed me in a rather stern voice that I would be allowed to receive one email a day and respond with another email. She enforced it, too.

My wife called my boss down in Southern California and explained the situation. He promptly took action which, if it was known to his superiors, might've gotten him fired. He produced a round-trip ticket for her to go to Napa immediately. He also sent me a rather stilted email which advised me that my request for a month's leave had been granted. I had not asked for a month's leave, of course. The reason was that he knew that the company we worked for would immediately want to lay me off once they heard that I had suffered a heart attack. I love that guy.

While I was in the hospital I had a couple of interesting incidents. The first one came when I was told to lie absolutely flat on my back — not even a pillow — for the first 24 hours. The gurney I was resting on was extremely soft and gave me a backache. I finally managed to get hold of a nurse and asked her if she could give me something for the back pain; I had in mind something like two Tylenol. She reached up and turned a valve. I had just enough time to ask her, "what's that?" The answer was, "morphine." It was a wonderful sensation and I slept for another 18 hours. I can see why people get addicted to it.

When I came out of it I looked around and I noticed that at the door of the room there was a prison guard. I knew it was a prison guard from our prison ministry; it's a distinctive uniform. I immediately began to think, "what did I say when I was under the anesthetic?" When the nurse came in next, I asked her just that question. She explained to me that the patient in the next room over was an inmate. California law required that a prison guard be with him at all times he was off the premises of the prison. Sadly, she also informed me that he probably was not going to survive whatever surgery was scheduled. She told me that inmates arrived in such a condition that they had waited too long for remedial surgery.

After the stent was put in, I felt much better. For another month or two I had the consistent experience of getting up, feeling great, putting in 10 minutes of work and then going back to bed. I was going to carry the bags up to the airline counter. My wife stopped me and pointed at the skycap pushing a wheelchair. She who must be obeyed indicated that I was to ride in the wheelchair and the bags would be taken care of. This is a form of wounded pride; us macho types know we can do anything. It helps some times to tell us, "no you can't." I wound up taking a month off teaching our the Bible class. When I got back one of the ladies in the class, a nurse, told me she was boycotting the class until I had been out 6 weeks. That was the period of time she felt was necessary for recovery. And during those 6 weeks, my pride took a beating. Sometimes God's got to do things the hard way to get things through your skull.

Moral of the story: Sometimes what you call suffering God sees as shaping you into the Christian he needs.

Grandfather's Money

My wife's father was, for most of the time I knew him, a wealthy man. He was also a very charitable man in the matter of producing scholarships for deserving students. What was interesting about them was that the scholarship paid everything, for as long as the student was in school and maintained a B average. He also did this for my children, so I have reason to thank him for that.

I probably discussed money with him more often than most people, because when we had first met he explained his "lease with option to buy" method of financing real estate. When he started the conversation, I remarked that I couldn't see how anyone would make money on that. When we finished, I remarked that I couldn't see how anyone could lose money on that. He concluded therefore that I was a very brilliant person.

Money has an effect on some people. In his case it became the driving force in his life; he needed to make more money. The result of this was that he alienated most of his family from him and found it difficult to have social relations with others. Betty and I occasionally brought up the fact that he was owned by his money, and he usually responded by telling us that he was proud of it. At the end of his life, he went broke. That was quite an adjustment on his part — and on ours.

Keep deception and lies far from me, give me neither poverty nor riches; Feed me with the food that is my portion, That I not be full and deny You and say, "Who is the LORD?" Or that I not be in want and steal, and profane the name of my God.
(Proverbs 30:8-9)

Laurian's Children

One of the heroes in my life is a lady named Laurian. She worked for me as a network engineer. One day my boss's boss came to meet this new employee. The interview went well until she asked how many children Laurian had. She replied that she had four children. The manager then exploded in anger, accusing her of wasting the planet, contributing to population explosion and several other sins of the ecological sort.

Interestingly, Laurian never got to tell her about those kids. She said she had four, but two of them were not her biological children. They belonged to her sister, who was incarcerated with a lengthy sentence for drug dealing. Laurian had taken the kids in, at her own expense, and was raising them. I don't know how you feel about the ecology movement, but surely it should have room for love.

Moral of the story: Do the right thing even if it's an ecological disaster. Love is greater than ecology.

Brain Surgery

One of the things that will drive parents nuts is having your child in a situation with serious consequences, and all you can do is wait for results. My daughter Rebekah gave us just exactly that experience. When she was a baby, the plates in her skull started to close up too soon — a condition which can result in serious brain damage. I want you to picture how my wife and I felt as we sat outside the operating room. I learned a few things there. One of the things I learned was that God sometimes takes his time, but when he brings comfort it's what you really needed. The pastor from our church came down and stayed with us all day. He didn't just "check in."

As you can imagine, we were greatly relieved when the doctor announced the operation was a success. When something you love is in danger, all the masculine impulses rise up. And then have nothing to do.

Moral of the Story: God has his ways of teaching you to wait upon him. So, I say, wait upon the Lord and He will renew your strength.

Plumbing Problems

We lived for a short while in a house owned by my wife's father. She agreed to move in on the condition that we replaced the non-functional garbage disposal. So picture this: three guys, each with a masters degree (economics, engineering and physics) are trying to remove the old dispoal. The unit came out quite easily – but the flange was rusted on tight. We hammered and sawed for quite some time until the guy with the masters in economics said, "I think we three combined earn more per hour than a plumber. Let's call one." We did.

The plumber arrived. He pulled out of his tool kit a small Sears sledgehammer – identical (even the same color) to the one we'd been using. He pulled out a Sears hacksaw – identical (yes, the same color) to the one we'd been using. He made two cuts in a direction we never thought of, hit the flange twice with the sledgehammer. The flange fell off, and he proceeded to install the new disposal.

Moral of the story: Sometimes it's not what's in your toolkit that counts. Sometimes you need to know how to use the tools, too.

The "Z"

At one time in my business life I worked for Nissan Motors, the people who import Nissans from Japan (formerly Datsun). Like most men of the time I thought it would be wonderful to have a 280 Z as my personal car.

As Christmas approached, my wife asked me what I would like to have for Christmas. Indulging in chaff, I answered her that I wanted a cute blonde in a short red dress with really high heels. She sighed, and then asked what I wanted second-most for Christmas. I told her at 280 Z at which point she gave up.

However, as it happens, about three days later we were driving down the street and saw the picture perfect example of the cute blonde in the red dress and high heels. I pointed her out, and my loving wife leaned over to me and whispered, "You're not getting the Z, either."

Moral of the story: Prepare your Christmas gift list early — and be reasonable about it. Sometimes it really helps to know what you really want.

Family Ties

Introduction

These next tales really belong to my mother and my father. I thought them so important, however, that I've included them in their own little section. The story about the walls is secondhand from my dad; and of course all his reminiscences about his father, my grandfather, come from him as well. I was there at Adak, but of course have no memories of it. But each of these stories has its importance, so I wrote them down.

My Walls Don't Fall Down

In early 1971, the community in which my parents lived (Sylmar) was struck by a major earthquake. Disasters are memorable. My mother was greatly grieved that her grandmother's crystal pitcher had broken. The entire house was a mess, but that was the one thing that really upset her.

But we did have one highlight coming out of that earthquake. A couple of weeks after the quake hit, dad found an elderly Hispanic gentleman wandering around in his backyard. He went out to investigate and found that it was the guy who had built the brick wall around the backyard. The old man was saying, "terrible, terrible" and began to speak to his sons in Spanish. Dad finally figured out that he wanted to rebuild the wall. Unfortunately, with no insurance for earthquakes, he did not have the money to rebuild the wall. He explained that to the gentleman, and received this reply: "my walls don't fall down! We start Monday on repairs." He rebuilt the wall at no expense to us because - his walls didn't fall down. The man never lacked for a reference from that time on.

Moral of the story: Craftsmanship is pride in your work, not in yourself. Be a craftsman.

Grandpa Was a Pitcher

My paternal grandfather died when I was just a baby. I always cherished, however, the stories my dad would tell about him. Children seem to need their grandparents somehow.

One of dad's favorites was this. My grandfather had been a professional baseball player in his youth. He was a pitcher, and particularly fond of that bane of a hitter's existence, the curve ball. My dad would often find himself with a catcher's mitt on the receiving end. Granddad would tell him exactly where to position the mitt. He would tell him not to move it; the ball would arrive there. But the curve ball is deceptive; it appears to be going one way and then drops and goes another. Dad said it took him many curve balls in the stomach to learn to keep the mitt in place.

I have very few souvenirs from my father's father. The one I cherish most is a beer mug, broken sometime in the past and repaired, which has on it in script the name "Red." When I was a young child I had bright red hair, which explains the name. But it is possible that I have inherited something else from him. My grandfather was a Bible teacher. From what I am told, he taught the men's Bible class at the First Church of Christ of Findlay, Ohio for about fifteen years. The average attendance of those times was over 300 men each Sunday. I have done nothing like that, but perhaps his talent for teaching the Bible in some small measure was passed down to me.

Grandchildren are the crown of old men, And the glory of sons is their fathers. (Proverbs 17:6)

The Rev. Will Hendershot

When my father was discussing his family, one of the mysteries that arose was his great uncle, the Rev. Will Hendershot. We knew that he was a preacher of some sort, or at least a clergyman, but the family had no real information about him after he joined the ministry. It seems he went from place to place and nobody kept up with him.

That was the status until one day a lady in my father's office came in and showed him an old piece of paper. It seems that her mother was a major player in the Women's Christian Temperance Union, whose major goal was the prohibition of alcohol. Her mother had died recently, and as she was cleaning out the attic she came across a number of old "broadsides" — the term used in those days for what we would now call posters. One of those broadsides had the explanation.

If you will recall your history, you will remember the name Carrie Nation — the short, stout woman with an ax went about from bar to bar smashing whiskey bottles and beer barrels. In her time, she was quite famous. It probably would never occur to you to ask how she got away with that; after all, if I did that I would be arrested. The answer, it seems, was given in this broadside. The Rev. Will Hendershot was shown at the back of the bar with two Colt .45 six guns trained upon the patrons.

Moral of the story: tracing your family tree can be interesting. But it helps not to be too judgmental.

Learning to Drink

When I was 13 years old I took it into my head that I was old enough to drink alcohol. My father handled the situation in an unusual, but effective, way. He started out by putting out a bar towel on the counter, and then proceeded to lay out all the implements he was going to need in a very neat and orderly fashion. When everything was arranged on the towel in precise geometric order, he turned to me and asked, "What's your limit?"

"I don't know."

Without a further word, my father began to put away all the implements he had just taken out. He did it with the same care he used in taking them out. It was rather a formal process. When he had finished he turned and walked away without another word. I didn't get another opportunity to try again until I was in college.

Moral of the story: know your limits. Know when not to exceed them.

The Lady Will Take It

The Native Americans of the great southwestern desert in the United States have developed their own unique sense of jewelry. My wife has inherited from my mother a necklace. This is the story of how she got it.

Dad being in the Army during World War II, he was assigned to different areas within the United States. One of those areas was Los Angeles, so they found themselves driving across the desert. They stopped at a combination of restaurant and jewelry store, selling the local product. Dad was immediately attracted to the necklace, and asked mother for her opinion. The price tag was twenty-five dollars. Remember, at this time a private in the Army made $18.75 a month. So, this was a fairly expensive necklace. She told him she didn't want it; it was too much money.

The two of them kept on looking, but dad went back to that counter, making sure that mom was nowhere near. He said to the clerk, "the lady will take it." He paid for it and put in his pocket, and about 200 miles down the road he pulled it out and gave it to her. Mom gave it to my wife before she died; the sentiment attached is a far greater value than whatever the piece is worth.

Moral of the story: Every gentleman should have a sense of elegance when giving to his love.

Tales of Adak

For most people, knowing where they were born tells you a bit about them. Some people are proud of where they were born; others are proud to be from where they were born. Your author was born on the island of Adak, Alaska on September 6, 1947. I was the 13th human being ever born on the island in all recorded history. The Aleuts were smart enough not to live on that island.

How did my parents get on that island? The answer starts back in World War II. The Japanese invaded the Aleutian chain of islands, taking two of them, Attu and Kiska. The United States Army established a base on Adak to manage the process of evicting the Japanese. At its height, the base had over 20,000 men — and precisely zero women. So, let's look at life on Adak as seen through the soldiers who lived there. The cartoons are taken from the camp newspaper and I think they give you a fair idea of what life was like.

"There's a lot of no place to go out here."

It was a frozen island stuck between the Bering Sea and the North Pacific. There was very little to do outside of military things, and a lot of time to do them. Bob Hope visited there once, and never came back.

'If ya go by Message Center, drop this off, willya?'

Adak, in the original language, means something like "birthplace of the winds." Weather was uniformly terrible to bad, and winds of over 100 miles an hour were common. Most of the time the winds were accompanied by fog which made for some interesting conditions.

"D'you know where th' hell you're goin', bub?"

Of course, with no women on the island, the stork's presence was unnecessary. At the end of the war it wasn't uncommon for most of the men on the island to have been there for over two years without having seen a female human being.

Into this environment in 1946 the government decided to ship up a few wives of some of the personnel on the island — including my mother. She had the unusual experience of being greeted at the dock by over 18,000 men.

I left the island early in my life with some medical difficulties which were beyond the capability of the local hospital. They flew me out to Seattle and things went from there. I have never been back to the island of Adak.

Moral of the story: If you can't be born someplace wonderful, at least be born someplace interesting.

Quote Unquote

A bit of explanation: there are several expressions that we have adopted as our own in this family, things you would hear us say fairly frequently which might not be obvious to the listener. Here are a few of them, with explanation.

Put it in the bag, troop

One of the expressions that we use in our family is this: "Put it in the bag, troop!" It comes from an episode in basic training as our supply sergeant was attempting to get us all the items we needed, with everyone getting everything, and doing so to prevent any possible mischance.

His method was quite simple. He would take one item that you were supposed to have, hold it up and wave it around, and then say something like, "everybody show me a tent peg." When he saw that all hands were up and waving a tent peg he would then instruct us, "Put it in the bag, troop!" If you do this for 100 or so items, the repetition becomes absolutely hilarious. It's been a phrase in our household ever since.

I won't say anything more, but I will say this.

Sometimes your own words come back to haunt you. My dad was one of those people who believed in a good chewing out. But every now and then he got a little carried away, and one night it came back to haunt him. In the middle of his diatribe, he said this: "I won't say anything more, but I will say this." He never got the next sentence out, and from then on out had to endure the chaff of us repeating that remark.

Up with which I shall not put

This expression comes, believe it or not, by way of Winston Churchill. Legend has it — and it definitely is legend — that Churchill, in one of his broadcasts, ended a sentence with a preposition. Specifically, he is alleged to have said, "this is something I shall not put up with." The grammatical rule of the time said that you never end a sentence with a preposition; "with" is a preposition. Supposedly he was chastised for this in a letter written from some Royal Society.

So, in his next broadcast, he mentioned the letter and, as he still had concerns about the original item discussed, asked to be allowed to rephrase it. He then said, "this is something up with which I shall not put." At least, that's the legend.

We use it a little differently. We mean something that's a minor annoyance over which too much fuss is being made.

You take care of the troops; the troops will take care of you.

Wisdom, like gold, is where you find it.

When I first became a manager in my business career, my father decided to give me some assistance. He took me into his bedroom, opened an old World War II vintage footlocker, rummaged around a bit and found a field manual entitled Small Unit Leadership. He handed it to me and said, "you're going to need this."

I took it respectfully, and made a mental note to myself that I would have to read it someday. Actually, I read it fairly soon after, and found that most of the manual was rather hokey. However, there were two passages which my father had underlined. At the margin he had written a note to each of these passages with the words, "all NCOs will read and initial." So, I figured these must be the two things that dad really had to say about leadership. Those two things are:

– Leadership is not a popularity contest.
– You take care of the troops; the troops will take care of you.

Those two precepts have gone a long way with me. I've always made it a point to make my decisions without worrying about whether people were going to like it. But I've also made a point of making sure that I take care of my people. My experience is that these two things, working together, are part of the essentials of leadership.

Right out of a Cracker Jack box

Every now and then my wife is called upon to perform some minor act of first-aid. These things usually involve a Band-Aid and some ointment of some sort. In the process, my wife will tell you that she got her medical degree out of a Cracker Jack box.

We have generalized that expression to mean that whatever it is we're doing is being done by a rank amateur, trying his or her best. We also use it to describe people who are completely incompetent at what they do, usually saying something like they got their PhD out of a Cracker Jack box.

All the seagulls you can catch

This expression means that you're chasing after something which just is not going to be caught.

It comes from an instance when my son was about three years old. We took him down to the ocean and went out on one of the fishing piers. He noticed that there were dozens of very large seagulls. He decided he wanted one. So, we told him he could have all the seagulls he could catch.

Give the boy some credit; he was persistent at it. But after about ten minutes, he figured it out: the seagulls did not wish to go home and become somebody's pet. We use the expression nowadays to let the air out of somebody's impossible dream quest.

Burst of Beaden

This is a spoonerism. It fell out of the mouth of one of our friends at UCLA, in our near campus Bible Study It was supposed to be "beast of burden." It's generally used in a mocking way, proclaiming to grandma how it is that I am totally overburdened and wearied of the great load I am carrying.

Eagles to Fly

There are any number of people that I have encountered who tell me that I have no idea how to raise children. Let me give you an example: when my boys were teenagers, their grandfather bought them each a car. You would think with that their father would have at least the sense to set a curfew. I never did.

What I did instead was to ask them what time they would be back, and at what time we should start worrying. It reflects our philosophy in raising children: we are raising eagles to fly, not chickens for Colonel Sanders. It seems to have worked; we have three eagles.

Days and Days

This one comes from my granddaughter. When she was about five years old, we visited them, in part to allow my daughter-in-love to go to a meeting in Washington DC. Lillian thought this meant that both her parents would be gone, so when we arrived she greeted us with a rather desperate question. "Mommy and daddy are going away for days and days; will you be here to take care of us?"

The Tummy Bongoing Duck

When our children were little, we used to amuse them with the Tummy Bongoing Duck. Using your hand imitate the duck, you raise it high above the child's stomach and begin to make noises like a World War II dive bomber circling at altitude. Then, swiftly, the noise changes to a dive bomber in full dive and when it arrives it bongos the kid's tummy. This usually produced a gale of laughter, and the kids would ask for it again and again. A similar creature was the Dive Pookying Duck, who loved to eat belly button lint.

The kids have long since outgrown this, but every now and then you'll hear grandpa threaten grandma with one of these creatures if she doesn't roll out of bed.

Insanity doesn't run in this family. It gallops.

Unabashedly stolen from Cary Grant in the movie *Arsenic and Old Lace*. I will leave to you the delight of finding the movie and watching it; it is one of the finest screwball comedies ever made. When you see the movie you'll understand how important it was to his character. In our instance, when we encounter events that seem more than usually bizarre, this is what we use to describe the situation.

Highlights at five; film at eleven.

Taken from a television station in the days when film was used for newscasting, it's an answer to a complaint. Originally used to announce something of importance, we use it to let someone know that their complaint is trivial.

It is intuitively obvious to the casual observer

Originally taken from a physics textbook, the thought was that the item in question was obvious and needed no explanation. We use it in the opposite sense; it means that whatever it is we're talking about is so arcane, so unrelated to the real world that it must be intuitively obvious. Or at least, that's the way we're going to treat it and we're not going to explain it to you.

Don't do dumb things

This one came from my mother. When I was about thirteen, she had the habit of listening to my wild-eyed schemes and plans. She would then dissect them piece by piece and logically show how the result was dumb. Then she would look at me and say, "don't do dumb things!" We use it pretty much the same way.

I'm SUCH a genius!

Stolen shamelessly from Wile E. Coyote, the phrase is very useful when you've done something very dumb. Sometimes, even, when somebody else has done something dumb.

Fred is a good name for a dust bunny

This one came about in a rather unusual way. Betty was complaining about the amount of housework she had, and used an expression to describe it. She said that if she didn't get the housework done, she was going to have to give the dust bunnies names. With a smile of innocence, my son David looked at her and said, "Fred's a good name for a dust bunny." Ever since then we've used it as a generic excuse for not doing the obvious.

I just do 'em; I don't explain 'em

Another comic theft, this one from Red Skelton. His show was on live for many years, and one evening he had the privilege of showing his flexibility. He told a joke (I don't remember it) and after the audience laughter had died down and it got silent again he tried the next joke.

Suddenly, a lady in the audience got the previous joke and laughed loudly. Skelton looked at her and said, "Look lady, I just do 'em, I don't explain 'em." Useful in all sorts of situations.

Thank you for sharing that

This one comes to us courtesy of Pirate Grandma Betty's tour of duty as a playground aide. Young children have an especially precious gift of being able say something totally inappropriate at just the wrong time. When this happened, the staff was directed to say "thank you for sharing that." It made the child feel that they were not being rejected, and if you could stifle the laughter it gave you a funny thing to tell your husband when you got home.

No one is ever a total loss - they can always be used as a bad example

Well, if you have read through this book so far, commenting to yourself what a horrible autobiography this is, then you now have one of those bad examples, don't you?

Of Influence

Winston Churchill

When I was about thirteen years old my uncle in Arizona gave me a hand-me-down set of Winston Churchill's History of the Second World War. What amazes me to this day is that better than half the writing in this six-volume series is taken directly from Churchill's memos. The man could write. He also could explain things in very simple and direct ways. I'm certainly not in his league as a writer, but it really helps to have an example like that.

CS Lewis

Any Christian born after World War II could tell you who CS Lewis is. Lewis is the most influential Christian writer of the twentieth century — and when you consider that includes GK Chesterton, that says quite a lot. His *Miracles — a Preliminary Study* is a masterpiece of apologetics. His clarity extends to his fiction; The Chronicles of Narnia, though not in the same league with J.R.R. Tolkien, is an excellent fiction series. In everything he writes you can see the influence of Christian thought. He is quite persuasive, and does not mind having to deal with the more difficult questions. It is his tough, intellectual honesty that makes him so worth reading.

Chrysostom

If you're going to read Chrysostom, you need to be acquainted with St. Vladimir's Seminary Press. In their "popular patristics" series you will find several by Chrysostom. I am told he is considered the finest preacher in the Greek language ever to grace the church. What I find interesting is that his sermons, written in a time of great controversy in the church, don't engage in political debate. They cover the practical side of Christianity. If you read nothing else, read his *Marriage and Family Life*. It is a refreshing contrast to the radical feminism espoused today.

Athanasius

Again from St. Vladimir's, Athanasius is more or less the opposite of Chrysostom. He is the guy who defended our version of the Trinity, as we understand it today, against the Arian heresy. He's also the person who formalized the list of books of the Bible that we now have. If you get his work on the Incarnation, there are two things of advantage added to what he wrote. One is the forward by CS Lewis. The other is his *Letter to Marcelinus*. It is in this that he explains that the Christian is closest to heaven when chanting the Psalms — or as we would say today, singing hymns — because only then is the Christian praising God with all his heart, soul, mind and strength. His masterwork is *The Incarnation of the Word of God*. St. Vladimir's has it under its Latin equivalent.

Thomas Aquinas

The greatest philosopher the church has ever known. His masterpiece, *The Summa Theologica*, is a work of sheer genius. I cannot pretend that I understand it all — but it is worth all the effort you can give it. You might also consider his *Catena Aurea*, the "Golden Chain." It is his verse by verse commentary on Matthew and Mark by all the important thinkers up to the time of Thomas. He wrote this from memory! It's out on the Internet somewhere.

Dorothy Sayers

As much as I respect CS Lewis, I have to say that Dorothy Sayers is the better theologian. She is every bit as good a writer; in fact, she's the one who wrote the Peter Wimsey mystery stories — and very good stories they are too. But among her many written masterpieces, the one that had the greatest effect on me was her Mind of the Maker. It is the most superbly simple explanation of the Trinity I have ever encountered while at the same time being the first and only explanation of the theology of creative art.

Thomas à Kempis

I picked up his *Imitation of Christ* at a garage sale for all of ten cents. All I can tell you is that that was the best dime I ever spent. It is broken into short essays, each of which will take you no more than ten minutes to read. But his thesis — that the individual Christian should be responsible for imitating Christ and therefore should read his words — was crucial to the beginning of the Protestant Reformation. He himself had no such intention; he just pointed out the obvious. If you decide to get a copy, I suggest you go with the one from Penguin Books. Superb reading!

www.ingramcontent.com/pod-product-compliance
Lightning Source LLC
Chambersburg PA
CBHW031408040426
42444CB00005B/468